The Wisdom of Dogs

Stanley Coren

BLUE TERRIER PRESS

The Wisdom of Dogs

Much of the material in this book originally appeared under the title of *What Do Dogs Know?* published in 1997. This is a revised edition that has been updated with additional content and new illustrations.

ISBN 978-0-9731052-9-2

ISBN 978-0-9936880-0-3 (Electronic Book Edition)

Contents

To my dogs, both the wise and the unwise:

Flint, Wiz, Odin, Banshee, Darby,

Skippy, Tippy, Penny, Feldspar

Dancer and Ripley

Author's Introduction

The book you have in your hands has a bit of a history that I'd like to share with you. Most of the books which I have written about dogs have contained a lot of material based upon the current beliefs of scientists about how dogs think, learn, and sense the world. Back in the 1990s it occurred to me that it might be fun to have a more casual book, one written with a bit of humor and an occasional bit of philosophy, some histories and even a bit of folklore, mixed in with all of that science. The idea was that each chapter would consist of a series of short interesting items that would be written in a lighthearted manner and connected by some personal observations. In addition the book would contain a number of illustrations to go along with the material.

Exactly what this book would look like was shaped through discussions with a wonderfully talented woman named Janet Walker. She was a fine artist who had illustrated *The Intelligence of Dogs*. Janet had also shown me a number of her marvelous, fun-filled drawings of Airedales and it was obvious that she should be chosen to illustrate the book. Together we produced the manuscript of *What Do Dogs Know?*

However, when the book was accepted for publication by Free Press, that acceptance came with some restrictions. The marketing people at Free Press decided that they wanted an avant-garde style of drawing, using a well-known artist whose style had become familiar through the numerous drawings that he had done for the *New Yorker Magazine*. They believed that this artist's popularity would add to the sales interest in the book. So in the end, as the title page indicated, it was "Illustrated by Pierre Le Tan" with "Illustrations inspired by Janet Walker." Pierre did a fine job, but it was a definite departure from what I had originally envisioned. In addition they decided that the book was short enough so that it could be compressed downward in size, using smaller pages and a small type font, and then marketed as a "stocking stuffer" or a casual gift for the upcoming Christmas holiday. The intention was to make the book look "cute" and there were no plans to have the book continue in further printings as a paperback.

I was always fond of this book, and was sorry that a version of it was not to be released to a broader audience. It has now been more than a decade and a half since *What Do Dogs Know?* appeared, and I have decided that perhaps it is time to bring it back and allow a wider public to share the humor, philosophy, and science about how dogs think. But of course since its original publication many things have changed. We are much smarter and more knowledgeable about how dogs think and how their minds work. So the book that you are holding is a revised and updated version of the original. There is new material in here and various parts have been rewritten to reflect the way that research has changed our view about dogs. In addition there are a whole new set of illustrations which I have drawn myself, and which I hope that you will find amusing and interesting. There were enough changes overall, that it seemed to warrant release under a revised title, hence the birth of *The Wisdom of Dogs*.

Whether you're a new reader or a returning dog aficianado, I hope you'll find something here to enjoy!

Stanley Coren

The Wisdom of Dogs

What do we know about dogs? As a Behavioral Scientist and Dog Trainer, who has spent many years studying dogs, I can say that we know quite a bit about their behavior, history and mental processes. Unfortunately, what we know about dog's mind is not always as clear and unambiguous as we would like it to be.

For instance, where do dogs come from? Scientists claim, each with a reasonable degree of certainty, that dogs may or may not have begun as domesticated wolves. Dogs may or may not be derived from jackals. It is also true that dogs may or may not have descended from the same distant ancestor that produced coyotes, dingoes, foxes and African wild dogs. Of course some combination of all of these is also possible since every one of those "wild species" can successfully cross-breed with dogs, and get perfectly sound (although often bizarre looking) puppies.

We know that for at least 14,000 years dogs have been partners with humans. Before that, dogs tried to establish an alliance with Neanderthal man. Neanderthals were not exactly stimulating company, but early dogs thought that they might be better companions than anything else available on the Earth at the time. When humans evolved into Cro-Magnon man, dogs immediately sensed a real potential in the new improved human model.

Some authorities have speculated that when Neanderthals were abandoned by dogs and left to shift for themselves, they became desperate and tried to domesticate cats. This may explain why, shortly thereafter, Neanderthals disappeared completely.

Cro-Magnon man and dog made an excellent team, and before long they were grilling antelope steaks over something called fire. Sometime later, the partners moved into caves and trapped the fire in something called a hearth. Once dogs had comfortably settled themselves in front of the hearth, the dog and human coalition was permanently established. Thousands of years later, when, so-called "civilized men" crossed the Atlantic Ocean and arrived on the shores of North America, they brought with them alcohol, syphilis, trousers, the bible and dogs. All were new to the native peoples—except dogs.

We know quite a bit about the way dogs' minds work, although far from enough to conclude that we actually understand the real wisdom of dogs. For instance, we know that dogs are intelligent. They are certainly smarter than horses, cats, dolphins and some politicians. The best guess is that the average dog is almost as smart as a two-year old child and maybe a bit better in toilet training skills.

We know that dogs feel emotions. They definitely feel

joy, fear and anger. Some experts claim that dogs may or may not feel guilt, grief and remorse. They also may or may not feel jealousy, ambition, humbleness, smugness or a desire to be a star in funny home videos.

We know that dogs understand language. The question remains, however, "How much?" One researcher claims that his dogs could only learn 22 words. Another researcher claims that dogs can understand 65 words. Further research suggests that there may or may not be 110, 165, 250 or up to 1000 words in a dog's vocabulary.

Dogs certainly learn the meaning of important words, like "walk", "bath" and "cookie", at least judging by the changes in their level of excitement when we say such things. This often causes people to spell out such words to avoid a frantic dancing anticipation or a dash for cover—but even then the dogs seem to catch on. I actually had a friend who resorted to using a second language when around their dogs, but after a while his perceptive pet caught on and effectively became bilingual. Along those same lines, I have seen a dog on television that sings "O Solo Mio" with better pronunciation of the Italian language than I can manage. Well, it may or may not be good Italian pronunciation since I know too little of that language to be a competent judge.

We are still learning about the complex interaction between dogs and humans. We know that dog's pact with man involves dogs giving up their freedom—but not giving up their independence. We also know that dogs are more loyal to their human friends than to their own convictions.

Given the state of knowledge that we humans have about dogs, perhaps it now time for us to assess the actual wisdom of dogs by asking "What do dogs know?" We can also ask some other important questions such as "What do dogs think about themselves?", "What do they think of those large two-legged dogs that they share their lives with?" and even "Do dogs have a philosophy of life?" In the pages that follow we will give you a set of facts, stories and simply some musings that may, or may not, answer some of these questions and help reflect the wisdom of dogs.

CHAPTER 1

How Do Dogs Think?

I have often watched my dogs when they were playing, resting or observing the world. As a psychologist I have seen evidence that dogs can think and reason and feel emotions, but what do dogs really know? What is going through a dog's mind as it is looking out of a window and observing the world? Near me now are four dogs, my two and the two that belong to my wife's daughter Karen. To the casual observer each appears to be watching and thinking. Some people say that they can tell what their dogs are thinking or feeling just by looking at them. To me it is obvious that Tessa is lying on the porch watching for intruders, ready to sound the alarm, as she always does. My retriever, Odin, is scanning the trees watching hopefully for birds. The youngest, Bishop, is slowly sneaking up on our cat, Loki. It appears to me that there is either play or malice in his mind. But then there is my inscrutable dog, Wiz. He is sitting and staring intently at a blank wall, his tail gently thumping on the floor as he gazes at nothing at all. This is common behavior for my old dog. Is he, like some Eastern Philosophers, contemplating the mysteries of the magnificent void or the purity of nothingness? Is he in some state of Zen meditation? Has he merely paused in this place to formulate his plans for the day? My wife passes by, looks at him, and comments "You know your dog looks like his brain has closed down again." Wiz thumps his tail once more. He may not be thinking—but he's happy.

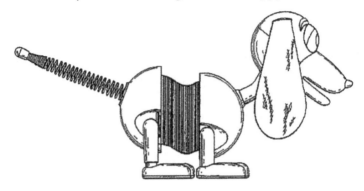

Some scientists believe that trying to analyze the wisdom of dogs is a foolish task since they are convinced that dogs cannot really think or reason. All of the behaviors that your dog engages in are therefore supposed to be done without thought, planning or insight. These experts still believe the theories of the French philosopher, Descartes, who would have described your dog as just some kind of machine, filled with the biological equivalent of gears and pulleys. This machine doesn't think, but it can be programmed to do certain things. Some say that Descartes had a hidden agenda. You see if dogs could think and if they do have consciousness, then, according to Church doctrine, they must also have souls. Anything with a soul is eligible for entry into Heaven, and some members of the Clergy were becoming concerned about possible over-crowding in Paradise. Machines, however, have no souls and therefore one need not allow a Beagle-shaped automaton or a mechanized Maltese to pass through the pearly gates of Heaven. As a byproduct, there would be no necessity to institute "Leash Laws" for dogs exercising on the Elysian Fields.

Some other experts feel that dogs are capable of reasoning and have the same kinds of mental processes that people do, although, perhaps, somewhat simpler in nature. For them dogs are almost equivalent to four-footed humans in fur coats. There are a number of cultures, including the Ainus of Japan, the Kalang of Java, or the Niasese of Sumatra, that have stories which claim that dogs are really the ancestors of humans. In some Tibetan monasteries a dog is brought into the room of a dying priest. The monks believe that the dog will serve as a temporary home for the soul of the holy man until he can be reincarnated in a new human body. Some religious sects go even farther and believe that dogs are actually people who will be restored to human form in the afterlife. Scientists, however, are in reasonable agreement that under a dog's fur coat we will find a dog.

It is certainly true that researchers have proven that the nerve cells in a dog's brain work the same as those in a human brain. The neurons that make up the human brain have the same chemical composition as the neurons in a dog and the patterns of electrical activity are identical. The structure of a dog's brain contains most of the same organs that are found in the brain of a person.

Just like in humans, dogs have special areas of the brain that are set aside for specific activities. In fact if we drew a map of the locations of various functions in the dog's brain it would be remarkably similar to the map for those same functions in the human brain. For instance, vision is located at the very back of the brain, in both dogs and people. Humans and dogs both locate the hearing part of the brain at the side of the brain, near their temples. The sense of touch and control of movements are in a thin strip running over the top of the brain for both dogs and people. However, if we look beyond the microscopic level there are some important differences between the brains of dogs and people. While Psychologists believe that as much as 60 percent of the human brain is set aside for processing conscious thoughts, interpreting and producing language, storing memories and solving problems, many dog owners believe that as much as 70 percent of their dog's brain is set aside solely to conjugate the verb "to eat"—in both the active and the passive forms.

Many of the ancient sages had a very high opinion of the dog's intellect and credited canines with great wisdom. The Greek philosopher Plato described the "noble dog" as "a lover of learning" and "a beast worthy of wonder". His contemporary, Diogenes, was another great Greek thinker, although a bit of an eccentric. Diogenes was known for wandering the world with a lamp while looking for an honest man. He thought dogs were extremely intelligent and even adopted the nickname "Cyon", which means "dog." Diogenes founded one of the great ancient schools of philosophy, and he and his followers were known by his nickname as "Cynics" or "Dog Thinkers". When he died the Athenians raised a great marble pillar in his memory. On top of the pillar was the image of a dog. Beneath the dog there was a long inscription that started with the following bit of conversation:

> "SAY, DOG, I PRAY, WHAT GUARD YOU IN THAT TOMB?"
> "A DOG."
> "HIS NAME?"
> "DIOGENES."

While the question of how intelligent dogs are is a matter of great debate among scientists, we do know that sometimes dogs can learn to do things that humans could never design programs to teach them to do. Take the rescue dogs that were named for the Hospice at the Saint Bernard pass in the Swiss Alps. The Saint Bernard dogs work best in teams of three or more. They are sent out on patrols following storms, and they wander the paths looking for travelers. If they come upon a stranded storm victim, two dogs lie down beside the person to keep him warm and one of them licks his face to stimulate the person back to consciousness. Meanwhile another dog will have already started back to the Hospice to sound the alarm and guide the monks to the scene.

The Saint Bernards are never given any special training, and no one is exactly sure how one would go about training a dog to do this task in any event. Young dogs are simply allowed to run with the older dogs on patrol. In this way the dogs learn what is expected of them. Ultimately, each dog decides for itself whether its job will eventually be to lie with the victim or go for help.

Sometimes people give dogs credit for knowing more than they actually do. Take the case of the Akita, named Kato, who was owned by Nicole Brown Simpson. Probably everyone on this planet knows that it was Nicole's murder, along with that of her friend Ron Goldman, which triggered one of the most public and controversial trials in history. Accused of these murders was sports hero and actor O.J. Simpson.

Kato enters the story because one of the neighbors heard the dog's agitated whining. It was then that the neighbor noticed that there was blood on Kato's feet, and thought that the dog had injured itself. As he went to return Kato to Nicole, the dog pulled in the direction of the garage. This was how the bodies were discovered. Many people felt that Kato had seen the murder and was trying to get help.

One morning, while O.J. Simpson's trial was in progress, I received a phone call from a lawyer associated with the court proceedings. He was offering a lot of money to get me to come to Los Angeles to meet with Kato and to see if I could somehow get the dog to help identify the murderer.

I tried to explain that, in comparison to humans, dogs have a mental ability similar to that of a two-year old child. I asked him if he would expect human two year old, with no clear understanding of death, and limited language ability, to be able to comment on an event that occurred nine months earlier. "Look," he pleaded, "couldn't you just come down and interview the dog?"

Forgetting that some lawyers are lacking in a sense of humor I quipped, "You mean something like getting him to bark once for 'yes' and twice for 'no'?" The amazed voice on the phone asked, "Could you do that?"

Another case of overestimating what dogs know occurred when I was asked to be the master of ceremonies for a series of dog demonstrations held at the Pacific Canine Exhibition. We had arranged for a number of "acts" including a dog that herded ducks, one that did scent discrimination, others that performed agility tricks, some that jumped and even a pair of dogs that danced with their masters. For comic relief we had Rupert, a loveable, lop-eared Basset Hound. I quickly taught Rupert that food treats might be found in several places around the stage. At various times Rupert would be released during another act. He would wander around leisurely, seemingly aimlessly, but really searching for the food. This served as the opportunity for some funny patter.

During the actual show, while a Labrador Retriever was demonstrating how he could catch three tennis balls in his mouth at once, Rupert sauntered across the stage once more. Having ingested quite a few treats by then, he stopped in the middle of the floor and emptied his bowels. The crowd roared with embarrassed laughter. Making the best of the situation I mock scolded him over the microphone "Now Rupert! Stop that and act like a gentleman!"

Apparently Rupert's bottom itched from the previous activity. He put his rear end down on the floor and, using only his front legs, dragged it across the stage and out of sight. The crowd laughed wildly so I improvised "Rupert, have you forgotten how to act politely?" at which moment he appeared again, going in the return direction, but still dragging his bottom across the stage. The auditorium collapsed in noisy giggles. After the show I was approached by two well-known Canadian dog trainers who told me they really were quite impressed. However, what they really wanted to know how I had trained Rupert to do "all that". Obviously I hadn't. Rupert was a "natural".

Scientists have shown that dogs think in concrete rather than abstract terms. One psychologist tried to see if dogs have any knowledge of mathematics, numbers or arithmetic. He made a series of little balls of hamburger meat and put them in groups in different locations on the floor. The number of meatballs in the groups differed, so that one might have a single ball, and another might have

3 or 4 balls of meat. He reasoned that if dogs understood the fundamental notion of numbers—such as "four is greater than one"—then given the opportunity to grab at a pile of meat, the dog would select the one with the largest number of meatballs. What this psychologist found was that when the groups of meatballs were at different distances, the dog was very practical. He simply grabbed the closest pile, regardless of its size. Only if there were two groups of meatballs at the same distance did dogs consider the number, and then they did grab the one with the most.

Even if dogs have the basic concept of size or number, it's a waste of time to ask your dog about higher mathematics. He probably thinks that geometry is some kind of new biscuit and algebra is some kind of three-cornered dog toy. And, when it comes to meatball-related equations, the most important concept appears to be "where's the beef"?

When older writers commented on dogs, they often referred to them as "dumb brutes". It is important to remember that the word "dumb" was being used to indicate an inability to speak and use language, not as an indication of a lack of intelligence. Dogs know that people often find it pleasant to come across someone who is not as bright or educated as themselves. It invokes in the brighter individual a feeling of love and protectiveness for the dull-witted one. For this reason dogs often cultivate a sort of a stupid, "I-don't-have-a-clue-as-as-to-what-is-going-on-around-here" look. Dogs feel that this makes we humans feel more superior and more relaxed around them.

Actually, dogs may be correct in their assumption since being ignorant with an equally ignorant friend can sometimes be quite comforting. For instance, I know that most of the philosophical discussions that I have with my dog are not very impressive, since neither my canine companion nor I knows what I am talking about. On the other hand, this fact does not stop me from enjoying the serenity and companionship that such discussions with my furry friend bring.

In the same way that human brain structure has much in common with that of dogs, the mental processes of dogs and people have many similarities. One mental process that dogs share with us is that they dream much the way that we do.

Of course, dogs dream only doggy things. We know this because there is a special structure in the brain that keeps all of us from acting out our dreams. When scientists have made that part of the brain inactive, they observed that the dogs began to move around, despite the fact that electrical recordings of their brains indicated that the dogs were still fast asleep. As these dogs moved they actually began to act out the actions that they were performing in their dreams. Thus researchers have found that a dreaming pointer may immediately start searching for game and may even start pointing at a dream bird, a sleeping terrier may start rapidly shaking his head as if he were killing a dream rat, while a dreaming Doberman Pinscher may pick a fight with a dream burglar.

You can tell when your dog is dreaming by watching him. When your dog first falls asleep its breathing will become more regular as the sleep becomes deeper. When the dream starts the dog's breathing becomes shallow and irregular. There may be odd muscle twitches, and you can actually see the dog's eyes moving behind its closed lids if you look closely enough. The eyes are moving because the dog is actually looking at the dream images as if they were real aspects of the world.

Not all dogs dream equally. It is an odd fact that small dogs dream more frequently than big dogs. A dog as small as a toy poodle may dream once every ten minutes while a dog as large as a Mastiff or an Irish Wolfhound may spend an hour between each dream. Just as in humans, the amount of time that dogs spend dreaming depends upon their age. Dogs spend more of sleep time dreaming when they are young puppies than when they are adults.

Some of the very large breeds of dogs, like the Newfoundlands, Saint Bernards and Mastiffs, often spend a great deal of their lives sleeping—perhaps up to 16 or even 18 hours a day. For this reason they were often referred to

as "mat dogs" because they could always be found lying in front of the fireplace, much like a giant furry hearth mat. If it is true that dogs dream about the activities that dogs do, then we must conclude that Great Danes probably only dream about sleeping.

There are old folk traditions that say that human dreams sometimes can be used to foretell the future. For people who believe in such forecasting techniques, dreams that include dogs have special meanings. As in the case of most prophesies, the trick is to figure out the message conveyed by the dogs in your dreams. Small differences in the nature of the dream dog can have special significance, such as its color. Thus a black or grey dog in a dream is said to mean misfortune, a white dog can mean victory and a red dog with white markings can mean speedy recovery from an illness. Dreams about Dalmatians, since they are both black and white, mean that there will be many changes in your life or many friends and enemies. (Dreams about pink dogs likely suggest a bit too much imbibing before bedtime!)

Dreams about dogs barking are good luck, while dreams where dogs howl are bad luck. Dreams about growling and biting dogs means that someone you know can't be trusted. Dreams about a dog licking your face is supposed to mean love and good fortune—but open your eyes first to check to make sure....it might just be your own dog trying to wake you up in the morning!

CHAPTER 2

What Do Dogs Sense?

Dogs and humans obviously do differ in many ways. Some of the most important differences are in terms of their senses. This means that dogs perceive the world differently from people. For instance dogs have an incredible ability to read scents. If you could unfold the inner surface of the dog's nose (the part that contains the cells that allow the dog to smell) it would actually cover a surface area larger than the entire extent of the dog's skin.

Dogs read the state of the world through their noses and they write their messages to other dogs in urine. A dog's urine contains a lot of information about that dog. It smells differently depending upon the dog's age and health. It smells differently for males, females, and females in heat. It even smells differently depending upon the dog's emotional state. That means any place that dogs frequently stop at and anoint with their urine really becomes a sort of a dog tabloid containing the latest news items in the local canine world. While it may not contain installments of classic canine literature, it certainly will have a gossip column and the personals section of the classified ads.

When my dog is busily sniffing at a favorite post or a tree on a city a street frequented by other dogs, I sometimes imagine that I can hear him reading the news out loud. Perhaps this morning's edition goes "Mimi, a young female

Miniature Poodle has just arrived in this neighborhood and is looking for companionship—neutered males need not apply." or "Buster, a strong middle-aged German Shepherd Dog, is announcing that he is top dog now, and is marking this whole city as his territory. He says that anybody who wishes to challenge this claim had better make sure that their medical insurance is current and paid up."

Any discussion of dog's sense of smell ultimately leads to the great, imponderable, question about dogs. It is the question which nags at children and leaves their parents groping for an appropriate answer. It is, of course, "Why do dogs have wet noses?".

Scientists have lots of answers for this. One is that evaporation of moisture from the nose helps cool the dog. Another suggests that added moisture in the nose helps capture the odor carrying molecules and thus makes the dog more sensitive to odors. The most boring answer is that many dogs simply lick their noses with their tongues, thus wetting them.

There is a folk tale that gives yet another answer. It goes back to biblical times, to that whole sequence of events associated with Noah and his ark. After the rain had stopped falling, and the whole world was flooded, all of the life on the planet was inside of that ark. The dogs constantly patrolled the ark, checking on the other animals and just poking around, the way that dogs do. One day, the pair of dogs was taking their daily stroll and they noticed that the ark had sprung a coin-sized leak, and water was rushing in at a rapid rate. One dog quickly ran for help while the other dog gallantly stuck his nose in the hole to plug it. By the time Noah and his sons arrived to repair the hole, the poor dog was in great pain and gasping for breath, however a major disaster had been averted. According to that tale dog's cold wet nose is simply a badge of honor, conferred upon all canines by God, in memory of that heroic act.

For dogs, beauty is taken in by the nose in the same way that for humans it comes through the eyes. People often wonder why an otherwise, apparently sane, dog, would roll around in garbage or dung. Scientists say that this behavior might be an attempt at disguising the dog. This is a leftover behavior from when our domestic dogs were still wild and had to hunt for a living. If an antelope smelled the scent of a wild dog nearby, it would likely bolt and run for safety. For this reason wild dogs roll in antelope dung. Antelopes are quite used to the smell of their own droppings and therefore are not frightened or suspicious of a hairy thing that is coated with that smell. This allows the wild hunting canine to get much closer to its prey. However, dogs know that the real reason that they roll in obnoxious smelling organic manner is simply an expression of the same sense of aesthetics that causes human beings to wear loud and colorful Hawaiian shirts.

Compared to their sense of smell, dogs seem to pay a lot less attention to their sense of taste. It seems as if dogs believe that if something fits into their mouths then it should be treated as if it were food regardless of what it tastes like. In this, however, they are wrong.

There are several common forms of people food that are bad for dogs. Probably one of the worst is chocolate, partly because people think that they are being nice to their dogs by giving them a bit of chocolate as a treat. In addition, chocolates are everywhere during holiday seasons, and it is easy to accidentally leave an open box of chocolates on a low table, around the height of a dog's mouth. The caffeine and a related compound, theobromine, contained in a single, ounce and a half milk chocolate bar can make a ten-pound dog very sick. The darker the chocolate, the higher the concentration of these compounds. That same amount of dark baker's chocolate can kill that same ten-pound dog. Onions and garlic are also on the banned list of dog foods. The large amount of sulfur in these vegetables can destroy red blood cells in dogs, causing severe anemic reactions.

However, even things that are not food are candidates for being swallowed by dogs. In Australia an eighteen-month-old boxer named Kizzy had been eating poorly and the medications prescribed by her veterinarian didn't help. Looking for a second opinion, Kizzy's owners brought her to another veterinarian. Following an operation, the vet retrieved a twelve-inch bread knife from the dog's belly! Amazingly, there was no serious damage, and the last reports noted that Kizzy was recovering well.

Most people know that a dog's hearing is much more sensitive than that of humans, but they may not know that the nature of the sounds that dogs hear is also much different from that of people. Dogs can hear much higher tones than people. Even the most sensitive people can't hear above 20,000 cycles per second, while some dogs can hear above 45,000. That is the secret of the so-called "silent whistles" that are sometimes used to signal dogs. These are not really silent, but simply produce a sound at around 25,000 cycles per second—too high for human's to hear, but not for dogs.

Smaller dogs can actually hear higher tones than bigger dogs. It has to do with the size of their ears. Small ears are more sensitive to high-pitched tones because there is a sort of resonance in the ear which amplifies these high sounds. On the other hand, the dogs with big square, mastiff-type heads,  which includes the Saint Bernard, can actually hear subsonic tones. These are very low frequency sounds, which are far too low for humans to hear. Thus the Saint Bernard is able to hear the faint low frequency sounds made by people trapped under the snow by avalanches, which dogs with smaller heads cannot sense at all. Some can even hear the very low sounds made when a body of snow starts to move over ice or rock. This is why some Saint Bernards have been successful at warning people about an impending avalanche, many minutes before it is detectable by people.

One television program attempted to show that dogs were musical. It showed video clips of dogs howling while their masters played a violin, clarinet or piano. This reminded me of a film clip that I had once seen which showed Lyndon Baines Johnson, who was then President of the United States. He was sitting in the Oval Office of the White House, with a white mixed breed terrier named Yuki on his lap. Johnson was lustily singing a western folk song and was hideously off key. Yuki was accompanying him with yips and howls that were at least as musical as the cacophony made by the President. Another president, Franklin Delano Roosevelt, claimed that he witnessed a performance of one of the world's greatest musical dogs. In 1936, FDR invited the Golden Gloves boxing champion Arthur "Stubby" Stubbs and his pit bull terrier, Bud, to the White House. He later reported that while Stubby played the banjo, Bud sang a medley of Stephen Foster songs.

The truth is that dogs may not really like music at all, but they absolutely love the noise that it makes. If dogs were patrons of the arts they would instruct their composers to write music like Wagner's operas—only louder.

This is not to say that there is no sense of tone or song

in dogs. There actually is a certain musicality within all canines, which would include domestic dogs as well as their wild relatives. This shows up in their howls.

One reason why dogs and wolves may howl is out of loneliness. They are basically asking, "Is there anybody out there?" They also answer another dog's howl with, what we can call a "yip howl", where the long mournful howling note is preceded by two or three yipping sounds. This yip howl says, "I'm here." When the howls of one dog are joined by the howls of others it often turns into a joyous celebration. The dogs or wolves happily announcing their own presence and their camaraderie with others of their species in what might be termed a spontaneous canine jam session. This vocal performance may go on for quite a while and involve animals from all over a region or a neighborhood. It is during such a wild concert that canines show their musical sensitivity. Recordings of wolves have shown that a howling wolf will change its tone when others join the chorus. No wolf seems to want to end up on the same note as any other wolf in the choir.

While dogs far outclass humans in terms of their hearing, when it comes to vision, humans are considerably better off than their canine companions. Dogs can never know much about colors since their color vision is limited. For many years scientists had thought that dogs could only see the world in shades of grey. Recent research has proven that dogs do have some color vision. This research involved training dogs to discriminate between various colored lights. In such studies it was determined that dogs are not completely color blind, it is just that they don't see the world in as many colors as humans do. The evidence suggests that dogs can't tell the difference between reds and greens at all and probably see the world in shades of blue and yellow. The fact that the training in these experimental tests is extremely difficult probably means that dogs don't attach the significance or importance to colors that humans do. For instance, take an old brown sofa that a dog likes to curl up in, and reupholster it in a delicate light blue fabric. Suddenly the dog's family won't let him come near it any more. Dogs are unclear about the concept here. Is light blue dangerous or unhealthy for dogs?

One should not talk about the color vision of dogs without remembering the case of Bill Bowen and his guide dog, Bud. All that Bowen had was the scant remainder of some peripheral vision and he had been declared legally blind. That's why he needed Bud to guide him through his daily activities.

In 1984, Bowen was arrested for drunken driving. He was found in the front seat of a car that had been weaving erratically all over the road. When he was brought before a judge Bowen testified that Bud had actually been driving, and that he was only the passenger. The judge, who clearly knew a bit about dogs, was skeptical.

"The witnesses say that the car did stop when the traffic lights turned red, and started again when they turned green. How could Bud do that, since dogs are color blind?" the judge asked.

Bowen was unfazed by this question. "Bud has learned the positions of the lights", he said. "He knows to stop when the top light is lit and go if the bottom one is on."

The court case was just about to move to the next stage, when Bowen broke down and admitted that he had lied. He said that he had been drinking, and now he was ashamed for trying to frame his loyal guide dog, when it was Bowen, himself doing the driving.

"I still don't understand", said the judge, "if you are blind then how did you read the traffic lights?"

"Well", said Bowen, "That really was Bud. He was in the passenger seat and he just barked once to tell me the light was green and twice to tell me the light was red."

Generally speaking, dogs are not as visually oriented as people. They certainly do not have the fascination that people do with mirrors. Most young puppies will respond to their own image in a mirror the first time that they see it. Usually, they will lose interest in it after only a few minutes, and from that time on, they will completely ignore their own reflection as if it did not exist. On the other hand, some dogs seem to like to watch television. Recent advances in technology have actually changed the TV viewing habits of dogs. Older style televisions used a tube where a raster painted lines on the television screen that refreshed the image about 30 times a second. Because the eye of the dog is more sensitive to motion than the human eye such television images seem to flicker and probably appeared to be less realistic or even a bit irritating for canines. Newer, high definition flat screen televisions do not have that problem and seem to be attracting more four-legged viewers. In fact now there are special videos made for entertaining dogs and in some places one can even subscribe to a specialty TV channel for dogs.

The videos that are most popular with dogs are usually shot from a dog's eye level view, and they include such activities as watching a tennis game, chasing a cat, and looking at birds. When it comes to broadcast television programs, one survey found that, for dogs, the top ranked TV shows included The Great Race and Wheel of Fortune. Dog's all-time-favorite TV movies seem to be anything by the Marx Brothers, the Three Stooges and Bugs Bunny. A dog day-care center in New York (which operates under the name of "Yuppy Puppy") keeps their charges happy by continuously playing Marx Brothers films on floor-level TV screens.

Dogs also seem to have other senses that humans do not. Researchers think that dogs may be able to sense the coming of earthquakes, even before sensitive scientific equipment can. For instance, there was a sudden increase in the number of dogs reported to have run away from home in the few days before the most recent major earthquakes in San Francisco and Los Angeles. One dog expert suggested that this sudden exodus of family pets occurred because the dogs were sensing something that they wanted to get away from—presumably the impending cataclysm. Some scientists think that, perhaps, dogs have a means of detecting changes in the magnetic fields around them while others believe that their ears may be sensitive enough to actually hear the faint cracking and snapping sounds coming from the region of the earth where the pressure builds up before the quake.

In a similar vein there are reports of dogs becoming upset and agitated enough to seek shelter, long before their masters become aware of approaching tornados, hurricanes or tsunamis. That is what happened in 2011 in the city of Miyako, Japan, when Babu, a 12-year-old Shih Tzu saved the life of her 83-year-old owner Tami Akanuma. Although not fond of going for walks, on March 11th Babu not only insisted on being taken out, but then stubbornly refused to follow Tami's lead. He literally dragged her to a nearby hill in the direction opposite their usual route. Whenever the elderly woman was forced to slow down in order to catch her breath, Babu would look back and urge her mistress to walk faster until they reached a higher point on the hill. Minutes later Tami watched in horror as the lead wave of a massive tsunami struck. It flattened the district of Taro-Kawamukai where they lived, and destroyed their home with a wall of muddy water. It appears that Babu had somehow perceived the coming tsunami that her human owner was unable to sense. The small dog reacted in a way that saved both their lives.

Dogs can certainly sense other things that human's can't. Take the case of Harley, a golden retriever owned by Victoria Doroshenko. Harley seems to have incredible medical sensitivity. Victoria, you see, is an epileptic and Harley warns her of oncoming seizures long before his owner, or anyone else, can see symptoms. How he does it is not clear. Perhaps it is by sensing small behavioral changes, changes in her body condition, maybe even her brain waves. Perhaps there is some chemical change in her body before seizure, and that might change the way she smells to Harley. However he does it, he is a medical miracle. Victoria says, "Before I got my dog I was afraid and housebound. Harley gave me my life back." Harley is not alone. There is now actually a Seizure Alert Dog Association that trains dogs to act just like Harley.

Dogs can sense more than just an oncoming seizure. Richard Simmons is a Research Associate working on a

project supported in part by the U.S. National Institute of Health. He told me a story about Marilyn Zuckerman of New York and her Shetland Sheepdog, Tricia.

Tricia had developed the annoying habit of sniffing or nuzzling Marilyn's lower back whenever she sat down and the dog could reach it. Marilyn's husband looked and noticed that there was a dark mole around the location that Tricia seemed to be interested in. It seemed odd that the dog cared about this mole, but since it caused no discomfort Marilyn simply ignored it. Then, one spring day Marilyn was lying face down on her balcony in a bathing suit, simply enjoying the sunshine. Suddenly she felt teeth on her back. It was Tricia, who had apparently decided that that mole shouldn't be there and was trying to remove it.

Marilyn's husband suggested that there must be something odd about the mole if it was bothering the dog that much. More out of curiosity than anything else, Marilyn showed it to her doctor. Before the day was out, Marilyn was at the Cornell Medical Center where the mole was diagnosed as skin cancer—actually a virulent and dangerous form of melanoma which can be fatal if not caught early enough. Tricia's early warning probably saved Marilyn's life.

Simmons told me "It was because of stories like that we began testing dog's diagnostic abilities. Our preliminary data suggests that dogs can detect melanomas and several other types of cancer well before there is any other indication of a problem. Some dogs will show agitation the moment a person with cancer enters the room. " Several scientists have recently developed techniques which can actually train dogs to detect skin cancers like melanoma, or when given a chance to sniff samples of urine they can detect bladder and prostate cancers. Perhaps someday that report on your cancer screening may most appropriately be called "lab test" because the test was actually done by a Labrador Retriever!

Some people are also convinced that dogs have ESP and the ability to sense the spirit world. One British scientist suggested that dogs use this ability to sense when their owners are coming home. To demonstrate this he installed hidden video cameras in the homes of dog owners. Most of the time these cameras simply recorded the dog sleeping, however, spontaneously the dogs would get up and start to hover around the door or window expectantly waiting at just the time that their masters were returning home, but still well before the sounds of the family car or their owner's footsteps could possibly be heard. Sometimes the dogs became alert simply when their master was more than a mile away and just beginning to start for home. It was not just a matter of telling time, such as having their master return from work at a predictable time each evening, since these tests were often conducted on weekends or at irregular hours. Rather than ESP, some scientists have an alternative hypothesis. They believe the dogs involved in the testing were extremely active and were constantly moving around and looking out of the window. One suggested "The dog was always on the alert, checking doors and windows, so much so that it would have been unusual if he were not looking out of the window when his owner finally arrived at the house!"

According to folk traditions, the dogs with the highest degree of psychic ability are the "four-eyed dogs", which are light colored dogs with a dark spot over each eye, or black dogs with light spots over each eye. Even today, on the Aegean island of Icaria, there are some people who always take four-eyed dogs with them to warn them if they come near a Nereid. Nereids are sea nymphs who are beautiful but dangerous. On land they lure men to their deaths over cliffs, while on sea they lure boats dangerously close to rocks.

Do dogs have a special sense that allows them to find their way back to their family from wherever they may be? This is the basis of one of the most famous and loved of all dog stories, *Lassie Come Home*, by Eric Knight. In that tale, Lassie escapes from the Duke of Rudling's harsh kennel keeper and the idea of going home becomes fixed in her mind. So begins Lassie's journey. It will take many weeks, and will bring her from Scotland to Yorkshire, a distance of 400 miles.

While Lassie was fictional, Knight had actually drawn his inspiration from a newspaper article about a dog that had found its way home over a distance of several hundred miles. There are many such true stories. Consider, for instance, the story of Oscar, a four-year-old beagle owned by the Hutchinson family. In October of 1988 they moved from Niagara Falls, New York to Indianapolis, Indiana, leaving Oscar behind to live with a grandson who was fond of him. In May of 1989, seven months later, Oscar arrived at the Hutchinson's new home. He was thin and bedraggled, with sore, bloody stained feet, after travelling over 100 miles farther than the fictional Lassie. Most amazing was the fact that Oscar had never left his neighborhood in Niagara Falls in all of his four years of life!

How did Oscar find his way? Perhaps Eric Knight had it right when he wrote about how Lassie managed to choose the correct direction home: "Do not ask any human being to explain how she should know this. Perhaps, thousands upon thousands of years ago, before man 'educated' his brain, he too had the same homing sense: but if he had it, it is gone now."

63 percent of dog owners admitted that they kissed their dogs.

CHAPTER 3

What Do Dogs Feel?

Ask the average person how you can tell you whether a dog is happy or not and they will tell you to simply look at its tail—if the dog is happy, the tail is wagging. Unfortunately that is only partly true. Rapid tail wagging, where the size of the side-to-side swings are not very large is actually a sign of excitement, rather than of pleasure. It is when the tail wags with broad swings at a moderate to moderately fast rate that the dog is either trying to say, "I'm pleased" or "I like you."

Some tail wags have totally different meanings. For example, a slight tail wag, with the tail held at its normal height is usually given when greeting a person or another dog. It obviously can be interpreted as "Hello there", but it also can mean "I see you looking at me. You like me don't you?"

However, some tail wags are far from a sign of pleasure. Thus a slow tail wag, with the tail held lower than at usual height is a sign of insecurity that often shows up when a dog is working on a problem, trying to understand what is going on. During dog training I interpret this signal as "I'm trying to understand you. I want to know what you mean, but I just can't quite figure it out." Once the dog finally solves the problem, the speed and size of the tail wags will usually increase until it becomes the broad familiar happiness tail wag that we interpret as happiness, pleasure and confidence.

One way dog's tail wagging is similar to a human smile is that it is a social signal meant to communicate the dog's emotional state to someone else. Most of us think that the human smile is automatic and bursts forth when we are feeling good whether we are alone or in a crowd. Psychologists have used hidden cameras to show that humans usually don't smile unless there is somebody is around to see them. The one exception is the occasional smile that we get when thinking about somebody special,

when they are, in effect, present in our thoughts.

Using the same technique, psychologists have learned that dogs reserve their tail wags for something that is alive. This means that a dog will wag its tail for a person or another dog and may also wag its tail for a cat, horse, mouse even a moth. However, if the dog is alone, with nothing in sight that is living, it simply doesn't wag its tail. Thus, when you give a dog a bowl of food it will wag its tail to say, "Thank you. You've made me happy." However, the camera shows that if the dog walks into an empty room and then finds its bowl full of food, the tail wagging doesn't appear. The dog will certainly go to the bowl and will eat just as happily as it did when you were around, but there will be no tail wagging, other than, perhaps, a slight rapid excitement tremor seems to be impossible to suppress.

Evolutionary biologists have also noticed that many breeds of dogs, and also jackals, wild dogs, dingos, and some wolves have a distinctive white or dark tip at the end of their tails. These scientists believe that marking is designed so that the living things dogs wag their tails at can see the tail's motion more clearly.

Although people often have difficulty recognizing a dog's emotions, humans certainly seem quite content to express their own emotions to dogs. One odd piece of research showed that 63 percent of dog owners admitted that they kissed their dogs. Where you ask? Some 45 percent kiss their dogs on the nose, 19 percent on the neck, 7 percent on the back, 2 percent on the legs and 5 percent on the stomach. An additional 29 percent listed the place that they kiss their dog as "other". The researchers didn't ask where "other" was and I don't even want to speculate.

While 63 percent of people admit that they kiss their dogs, only 51 percent say that they allow their dog to return the affection by licking their faces. For some unknown reason, married men over 45 are the group least likely to allow this kind of loving to occur.

We can find physical evidence of our affection for dogs in our wallets or purses. Market researcher Barry Sinrod looked at the pictures that people carry in their wallets. It turns out that 87 percent of all people carry some kind of pictures. Of those, 75 percent carry snapshots of the kids and 55 percent have one of their spouse. Some 40 percent carry photos of their dogs, which is 20 times more frequent than pictures their mother-in-law, which were carried by only 2 percent of all the people surveyed.

A dog's mind can grasp the basic feelings such as joy, anger, fear and excitement. Yet there are some complex emotions that humans have that are quite foreign to dogs. One such emotion that dogs don't have is guilt. Perhaps the only guilt that dogs could possibly know is when they fail at their obligation to be true dogs. Dogs do not worry about morality, scruples, ethics, principles, standards or virtue. The pendulum of a dog's mind oscillates between "possible" and "impossible," not between "right" and "wrong." For instance, I had a Cairn Terrier by the name of Flint who was a continuous source of exasperation to my wife, Joan. She would shoo him off of a chair only to see him immediately jump up on the sofa. She would push him off of one side of the bed only to have him jump back up on the other side. She would scold him for barking at the door only to have him jump up and begin barking at the window.

One day when some company was visiting, Flint wandered around the room nosing at the visitors in the hopes that one of them might scratch his ear or perhaps drop a bit of food. With some concern that he might be annoying her guests, Joan waved him away saying, "Flint, stop bothering these people. Go find something interesting to do."

Flint took her at her word. He darted out of the room, only to appear a few minutes later carrying one of her undergarments which he proceeded to flagrantly snap from side to side with great joy—to the amusement of her guests and the dismay of my wife. As with many dogs, Flint's motto was, "If two wrongs don't make a right, try three."

One reason why dogs do not attempt to guide their lives by any ethical principles is because they know that the world is filled with duplicity. Dogs often feel that what is right today might well be wrong tomorrow, or what is correct behavior for some favored few is considered improper for unfavored majority. If you press dogs for an example they will demonstrate that what is considered immoral or criminal behavior in dogs is often the logical

extension of activities that are considered perfectly
respectable for cats.

Dogs know one aspect of human emotion very well.
They understand that they bring hope and comfort to
humans, just by being near them. A seaman who was with
the British Royal Navy during World War II told me a
story about a mixed-breed dog named Daisy, who proved
that.

Daisy was the mascot of a Norwegian trawler. She
spent most of her time in the wheelhouse, while the ship
was fishing in the North Sea. One night, without any
warning, a German U-boat torpedoed the ship. It was
blown to bits and Daisy, along with the remaining crew,
found themselves struggling to keep afloat in the darkness.
By the light of the burning wreckage survivors managed
to find each other, and they congregated in a little knot.
Daisy saw them, and swam over to join the huddled group.
Through the black night, Daisy paddled from one sailor
to another. She would stop, and appear to check on their

condition, and then she would lick the crewman's face.

A seaman from the ship that rescued them told me, "The survivors felt that she was reassuring each man, and telling them that they would make it if they only didn't give up. They had been in the water for several hours when my ship picked them up. We put them ashore back in England. All that they seemed to want to talk about was Daisy. They said that it was her presence that kept them going and kept their spirits up, even though they had little hope of being rescued." The Royal Society for the Prevention of Cruelty to Animals heard of this story and commemorated Daisy's courage and compassion by awarding her a medal.

Dogs do know fear. It is a useful emotion. It keeps them from trying to leap chasms too wide to breech, or trying to hunt semi-trailers on the highway. However, the greatest fear that dogs know is the fear that you will not come back when you go out the door without them.

Dogs also have a different perspective on friendship. When they commit, they truly commit. One of the oddest delusions that people have is the notion that friendships should be lifelong. The truth of the matter is that humans have flexible minds that continually transform themselves. Because of this, as people age and change, they wear out their friendships as they wear out their clothes, their political beliefs and their love for loud music. Only the friendship between a dog and a person seems to have the resilience to withstand these changes.

CHAPTER 4

What is Dog's Nature?

Dogs do not write, so there are no diaries to tell what an individual dog has learned. Dogs do not have museums and libraries, to display and conserve any erudition, culture and discernment that they have acquired as a species. Dogs simply store all of their wisdom in their genes. Even scientists are amazed at how much of a dog's behavior is genetically controlled.

Take the case of Dalmatians. These dogs were originally bred to run under a horse-drawn carriage, and then to guard it when it was parked (sort of the first car alarm). Fashion dictated how the dog was to run with the coach. The "ideal coaching position" was when the dog ran in a position under the front axle of the carriage, very close to the heels of the rear horses—the closer the better. Dogs that ran under the center of the carriage or under the rear axle were in "poor coaching position".

When Harvard University researchers looked at 25 years of kennel breeding records they found that mating two dogs which both ran in good coaching position was much more likely to produce a dog that also ran in a good coaching position compared to puppies from the mating of both a good and a bad coaching position dog. The worst dogs came from mating two bad coaching position dogs. The fewest cases were found in this last group since, as might be expected, the kennel had no interest in developing a line of Dalmatians that automatically assumed bad coaching positions.

Because so much of a dog's behavior, is determined by its genetic makeup, the specific breed becomes an important means of predicting an individual dog's nature. A dog's genes obviously determine the dog's breed and the essence of a "pure bred" dog involves controlling its genetic make-up through selective breeding. Knowing a dog's breed is a good way to predict the dog's activity level, intelligence and its personality.

For example spaniels tend to be the most sociable of dogs, followed by the retrievers. The working dogs, like the German Shepherd, the Doberman Pinscher, and the Collies tend to be sober citizens who are willing to be friendly, but don't like overt "kissy-face" kinds of behavior. Terriers tend to be feisty and standoffish and there are some breeds of hounds that are only barely willing to acknowledge that humans exist. One person once told me that he had a dog that was half pit bull and half poodle. He claimed that it wasn't much good as a guard dog, but it was a vicious gossip.

Generally speaking, the names of dog breeds are derived from the place where that dog breed was originally developed. Thus we have Irish setters, Labrador retrievers, Yorkshire Terriers, French Bulldogs and so forth. Less commonly dog breeds might be named after the person who developed that particular breed, such as the Doberman Pinscher or the Jack Russell Terrier.

Despite, the geographic appellation, spaniels are a group of dogs whose name actually seems to come from their temperament. The  word spaniel is derived from "español", which is the Spanish word for "Spanish". However none of the spaniel breeds was actually developed in Spain, or any of the Spanish-speaking countries. So why have spaniels been linked to Spain? The answer here comes from their temperament. Most of the spaniel breeds are incredibly loving. At the time when the spaniel breeds were first being developed, it was believed that the greatest lovers in the world where the Spanish, so obviously, a dog that is happiest when he is kissing your face must have a Spanish origin or association of some sort—even if in name only.

Each dog breed has its own unique characteristics and personality that make it special. For instance, there are owners and breeders who insist:

✖ The Airedale believes that it is of no use to anyone unless it provokes a furor.

✖ Each year a healthy Jack Russell Terrier consumes one and a half times his weight in human patience.

🐕 Bulldogs display that typically English characteristic for which there is no English name.

🐕 All Poodles act as if they have won first prize in the lottery of life.

🐕 The Labrador retrievers have a way of getting to the answer "yes" without ever having posed any clear question.

🐕 The Chihuahua's greatest ambition is to live in a hot country and watch their master throw stones in the sea.

🐕 If spaniels had a motto it would be "You've got a face, I've got a tongue, I'm sure we can work something out!"

🐕 Golden Retrievers are not dogs—they are a form of catharsis.

🐕 The beautiful and elegant Afghan hound knows two things: first that they are not very smart, and second that it doesn't matter.

The issue of a dog's personality probably also determines the popularity of the breed. It is interesting to note that the roster of the most popular dog breeds (in terms of the number of purebred dogs registered with the kennel clubs) has remained fairly constant. In the United States and Canada, over the last decade, the top 10 breeds of dogs have consistently included two substantial guard dogs, the German Shepherd dog and Rottweiler; two full-sized intelligent and friendly family dogs, the Labrador Retriever and the Golden Retriever; the elegant and adaptable Poodle; and a playful little hound, the Beagle. In a typical year the American Kennel Club will register over 30,000 litters of each of these breeds.

Some dogs go in or out of fashion depending upon their star status. Thus Lassie's TV adventures moved Collies out of pastures and into many living rooms. The Beagle's popularity has likely been forever assured by Snoopy's antics in the daily *Peanuts* comic strip. And whether Dalmatians are in the top 10 breeds or not largely depends upon how recently Disney Studios has released or re-released some version of the movie *101 Dalmatians.*

As of the time of this writing the 10 most popular breeds in the western world are

1. Labrador Retriever
2. German Shepherd
3. Beagle
4. Golden retriever
5. Yorkshire Terrier
6. English bulldog
7. Boxer
8. Poodle
9. Dachshund
10. Rottweiler

While the demographics (or "dogographics"?) are undeniably intriguing, dogs don't know many statistics about their kind. They are not like humans who seem to have a pressing need to take a census every few years and do a lot of counting to determine how their species is flourishing.

When humans extend their penchant for counting and try to figure out the exact number of dogs there are in the world they run into numerous problems. In many countries people don't keep dogs inside their homes as pets. In some places the dogs simply roam freely in the streets and, because nobody really owns them, counting is difficult. The best scientific guess is that there are over 400 million dogs in the world. To get an idea of how many dogs this is, we would have to add the total number of people in the United States, Canada, Great Britain and France to get as many humans as there are dogs in the world!

In comparison, the number of wolves in the world is a lot less than the number of dogs. Even if we add together all of the wolf species from all of the countries in the world we still only arrive at about 400 thousand individual wolves. In other words there are a thousand times more dogs in the world than wolves!

One reason why there are so many dogs has to do with the fact that a female dog can have her first litter of puppies when she is only five to 18 months old (depending upon her breed). It takes 58 to 70 days to have the puppies. The average number of pups is usually between six and ten. Every female dog can have two batches of puppies each year. Each of her puppies, if they are females, can also have pups when they mature. That means that one female dog and her offspring could produce 4,372 puppies in seven years! That's a lot of mouths to feed! But since dogs have not mastered the concept of child support none of this seems to matter much to them.

Despite the potential for a canine population explosion, some dogs have become extremely rare. The reason for some is almost paradoxical: they were too good at their jobs. Take the Scottish Deerhound, who was used to hunt a Scottish deer that could stand over five feet at the shoulder. When Scottish Deerhounds had hunted their prey to extinction, the breed lost its major function in life and its favor amongst hunters. And some venerable breeds with long histories, such as American Foxhounds, English Foxhounds and Otterhounds are teetering on the edge of extinction because of laws that restrict or ban the hunting of foxes or otters with dogs.

Other dogs have seen their popularity fade simply because their "star status" faded. The distinctive looking and rugged Dandie Dinmont Terrier owed its original popularity to Sir Walter Scott's book *Guy Mannering*. While it was a best seller in 1814, this book is virtually unread today and is a contributing factor to why we seldom see Dandie Dinmonts any more.

In some cases the diminished popularity of a breed is a fashion statement. Such is the case of the Irish Water Spaniel. Despite its working ability, intelligence and pleasant manners, to many people the Irish Water Spaniel merely looks like a bad Poodle with a rat tail.

Of the more than a half million pure-bred litters registered by the American Kennel Club each year, some breeds will account for only two or three dozen litters each. In fact, some recognized breeds of dogs are now so rare, that if they were wild animals they would probably be listed on the International Endangered Species List. For example a worldwide count of the number of Otterhounds managed to find fewer than a thousand dogs. Some endangered dog breeds include:

- Otterhounds
- American and English Foxhounds
- Irish Water Spaniels
- Dandie Dinmont terriers
- Scottish Deerhounds
- Harrier
- Sealyham Terriers
- Sussex Spaniels

Dogs certainly know more about their own breeding than do most humans. Take the case of Steven and Barbara Kaufman of New York City. On a European holiday they visited a small village near the Alps where a man offered to sell them a puppy from a litter of Tyrolean Mountain Dogs. The Kaufmans had never heard of this breed before.

The man then showed them the litter of puppies and explained that this was an extremely rare breed of dog that was bred only in this region of the world. He explained that "These grow to be quite large dogs, and their big wide paws and phenomenal strength give them the ability to climb mountains and deal with snow and ice conditions better than other dogs."

The Kaufmans fell in love with these honey colored tailless puppies, with their fat paws, blunt faces and round ears. The asking price was quite steep, however, this was to be expected for such a rare breed of dog. In addition they received an ornate certificate with their puppy's kennel name and breed. They named the dog Piton, after a piece of climbing equipment, which they felt was appropriate for a mountain dog.

Once back in New York they found that Piton was growing at phenomenal rate, and was eating quite voraciously. Piton was also becoming a bit aggressive especially when they tried to cut his quickly growing toenails. The Kaufman's thus decided to take him to the veterinarian for a nail trimming. When they hauled Piton onto the examining table Barbara proudly told the vet "I'll bet that you haven't run into many animals like this before." The vet nodded and said, "That's certainly true. This is the first time I have

been asked to treat anybody's pet bear!"

Sometimes it is very unwise to try to modify dog's nature. Dog shows are where beauty, physical soundness and conformation to breed standards are assessed. They were designed to identify dogs that are the best examples of their breed, so that the finest dogs can be bred to produce puppies with the most desirable characteristics.

Since the ability to breed is important, dogs that are entered must be intact (not spayed or neutered) and male dogs must have two normal testicles. A dog with only one testicle descended into the scrotum is called a monorchid, while one where neither has descended is called a cryptorchid. Either condition will result in disqualification. Fortunately, for some dogs, such problems correct themselves over time, and the testicles do eventually descend so that the dog can be shown.

There is a story, however, of a man who owned, what he believed was a particularly handsome young Rottweiler. Unfortunately it was a cryptorchid whose testicles had failed to descend. He wanted to enter this dog in a specialty show in Philadelphia in order to impress some friends. At great expense, he had a veterinarian put in testicular implants (for cosmetic reasons, he assured the vet). A couple of months later the dog was entered in the Philadelphia show. While in the ring, the judge was amazed to find that this Rottweiler had four testicles instead of two. Its owner had missed the fact that, just a few days before the show, the dog's natural testicles had descended to join the implants. The owner and his now too masculine dog were summarily ejected from the show.

The genetic makeup of dogs provides some breeds with special abilities. I recently received a phone call from the Royal Canadian Mounted Police which patrols the highways in the Province of British Columbia where I live. The RCMP constable told me that he was associated with the new automated photo radar system that was being introduced to control speeding on the highway. The system is designed to automatically measure the speed of vehicles passing the installation. If any vehicle exceeds the posted speed limit by a specified amount, a photograph is automatically taken, with a high enough resolution to read the license plate. The car's owner is later sent a traffic ticket and a copy of the incriminating photo on which their excessive speed was recorded. I was puzzled and asked why the police were contacting me about this issue.

"Well," he said in a rather uncomfortable tone of voice, "we set up one of the first monitors near an elementary school with a posted speed limit in the school zone of 20 kilometers per hour (around 15 mph). The first two speeders caught by the system were something that looked like an Afghan hound and something that looked like a Doberman Pinscher. We wanted to know whether this kind of speed was common enough in dogs to pose a problem for us."

Dogs certainly know how to run and many can reach speeds of 60 to 65 kph (35 to 40 mph) in short running bursts. Greyhounds can maintain a speed of around 40 mph for a distance of 7 miles. The fastest greyhound ever clocked was Ballyregan Bob, who could run a kilometer in 40 seconds, which is 90 kph (over 56 mph). But dogs are pretty canny; they know that as long as they are not wearing a license plate they will never be fined for speeding.

CHAPTER 5

How Do Dogs Speak?

One of the most controversial questions about what a dog knows has to do with language and communication. Do dogs understand our speech? My own research indicates that the average dog can learn about 165 words (well really that includes signs and signals as well) and the "super dogs", the ones that are in the top 20% of canine intelligence, can learn in excess of 250 words.

Of course there are savants, such as Chaser, a Border Collie owned by retired psychologist John Pilley, who apparently knows the names of around 1000 items. John often forgets the name that he assigned to particular toys and things that he asks Chaser to pick out, so he frequently writes the name on the toy itself under the presumption that the brainy dog Chaser can't read.

The evidence provided by Chaser certainly shows that dogs can understand a substantial chunk of human language. Yet this still leaves us with the question of whether dogs can speak. Dogs can't form word sounds very well because they don't have the special ability that humans have to control over their tongues and vocal cords. Dogs have only a tail to wag, ears to flap and a tongue to lick with, so it is unfair to expect them to create poetry.

Yet, in the absence of the spoken word, dogs do

communicate. When my dog sits and listens to me tell him about complex problems and then gently beats his tail against the floor, I know that this really means, "You're getting closer to the answer. Keep at it and I'll let you know when you're there."

One common belief that spans the world, and is held by many African peoples, Australian aborigines, Native Americans and Haitians, is that dogs can understand every word that we say. According to these folk beliefs, not only can dogs understand speech, but it is believed that dogs actually have the ability to talk under certain circumstances—if they have a particular reason to do so. For instance, there is an Irish legend that gives us the good news that there is a way for people to understand dogs if they talk. Dog's speech becomes interpretable only if the listener is standing directly in front of the dog while wearing a four-leaf clover. The bad news part of the legend is that these Irish dogs only feel the need to talk just before a disaster.

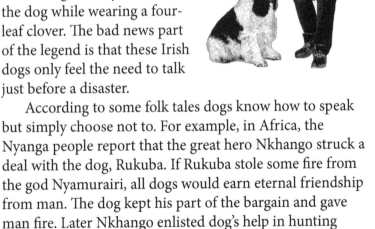

According to some folk tales dogs know how to speak but simply choose not to. For example, in Africa, the Nyanga people report that the great hero Nkhango struck a deal with the dog, Rukuba. If Rukuba stole some fire from the god Nyamurairi, all dogs would earn eternal friendship from man. The dog kept his part of the bargain and gave man fire. Later Nkhango enlisted dog's help in hunting and together they successfully killed such dangerous prey as the wild boar and even the lion. Because of the dog's intelligence Nkhango began to entrust him with even more tasks. Finally Nkhango decided to use dog as a messenger. This was too much for Rukuba. All that the dog really wanted was to lay by the fire in comfort. Since he had given humans fire, he felt that it was his right to do so. Rukuba concluded that men would always be sending him to this place or that on errands, because he was clever and could speak. Then the dog thought, "If I could not speak then I could not be a messenger." From that day on, the dogs choose never to speak again.

Unfortunately this did not save dogs from serving as messengers. The army of ancient Rome used dogs to carry messages between military units. Routine messages were placed in a small container attached to the dog's collar. Secret messages were treated differently, however. They were placed in a small metal tube that the dog was forced to swallow. Unfortunately for Rukuba's decedents, the process of retrieving these messages involved killing the dog and opening its stomach. Perhaps if these dogs knew what was planned for them they might have reconsidered their vow of silence.

The American Animal Hospital Association carried out a survey of people's attitudes toward their pets. One of their questions was "When you are away, do you ever talk to your dog on the phone or through your answering machine?" The questionnaire did not, however, ask people to tell them what their dog said in response to their phone messages.

Another published survey did directly try to answer the question as to whether people really think that their dogs are talking to them when they bark, whine or whimper. Based on over one thousand questionnaires, this survey found that 78 percent of dog owners think that their dogs are actually speaking to them. And what are these dogs saying? Actually the people questioned felt that their dog was telling them quite everyday things, like: "It's time to let me out", "I want a walk", "Let's play", "Come here", "My water bowl is empty" or "I love you". Not one respondent mentioned that the dog was providing comments on ancient oriental philosophy, politics, religion or the state of the economy.

The average person certainly acts as if they believe that their dog has a comprehensive knowledge of human language. Whether dogs understand our speech or not, they are wonderful listeners. One friend of mine tragically lost her husband just a few months after she learned that she was pregnant. She later admitted to me that talking to Gus, her Golden Retriever, was one of things that helped her through her crisis. "I could sit and talk to him and he would stay close and just listen. I told him what my plans were, what I thought I would do next, and how I was feeling. He would listen and then lean against me as if he wanted to reassure me. I think I interpreted the fact that he was listening, and not getting upset, or walking out of the room, as meaning that what I was doing was alright and what I was feeling was normal."

In our culture we don't find it all strange when people talk conversationally to their dogs. Consider one of the all time classic films, "The Wizard of Oz", where Judy Garland became a star by playing the role of the little girl from Kansas, named Dorothy. Actually, in that film nearly half of Garland's lines are addressed to Terry, the Cairn Terrier co-star who played the role of Toto.

Scientists accept the fact that dogs are good listeners, however they claim that the stories suggesting that dogs can actually talk are simply untrue. According to researchers, if your dog tells you that he can talk, he's lying.

Some people believe that dog's really don't understand words, but only respond to your tone of voice. Accordingly if Fido usually responds to "Fido, roll over" he will also respond to "Hi-ho, goal blubber." This may really reflect the dog's cleverness at being able to piece together the meaning of our often slurred and distorted speech. After all, when our mouth is full "Lassie, come!" is apt to come out as "Frassy, glum!", but our dog arrives at the table, nonetheless.

I have already told you about how researchers have proven that dogs do respond to specific words in laboratory settings. It was also proven more informally by the actor Richard Burton. Burton was married to actress Elizabeth Taylor, and they co-starred in several films, such as "Who's Afraid of Virginia Wolf?" and "Cleopatra." Taylor was so fond of her many dogs that once, when shooting a film in England, she insisted that they live on a boat moored on the Thames. Thus her dogs never needed to step on the English shore and avoided the usual period of quarantine.

Taylor felt that she could communicate better with her dogs than Burton could, and, somewhat to his annoyance, the dogs always responded more reliably to her words. This was the case until Burton brought her a Pekingese, named E'en So. The dog was blind in one eye and Burton claimed that he had "rescued it". Although the dog seemed friendly enough, Elizabeth Taylor could never get it to respond as well to her as it did to Burton. It seemed to ignore her words and only pay attention to his. Burton later admitted that he had purchased the dog fully trained, but only to commands spoken in Welsh—a language that he spoke fluently but which she knew not at all.

Sometimes dogs show unexpectedly good language comprehension. In the United States, the abolition of slavery came after a bloody civil war. If dogs kept a history they might recount that their own period of slavery ended with the invention of mechanical and electrical motors. Many dogs were specifically bred as compact sources of cheap power. For example, meat was traditionally cooked over an open fire on horizontal spits that needed to be rotated to cook the meat evenly. The tedious job of turning the meat was given to a special breed of heavy, long-bodied and short-legged dogs, appropriately called "Turnspits". They were placed in an enclosed wheel, like the suspended wheels that you sometimes see in hamster cages. The dog's walking generated the rotary motion needed to turn the metal spit which was attached to its center. A house might have several turnspits, and each might be required to work the wheel for a number of hours. Turnspit dogs were also used to generate the motion needed to churn butter, grind grains, pump water and there is even a patent for a dog powered sewing machine.

When turnspit dogs were not needed as a source of power, they were often taken to church to serve as foot warmers. One Sunday the Bishop of Gloucester was giving a service in Bath Abbey. He drew his text from the tenth chapter of the Book of Ezekiel. He turned to the congregation and shouted, "It was then that Ezekiel saw the wheel." At the mention of the word "wheel," the turnspit's dreaded work place, one witness reported that a number of dogs "clapt their tails between their legs and ran out of the church."

CHAPTER 6

What Tales Do Dogs Tell?

The Chinese zodiac contains only animals. One of these celestial animals is a dog, although we don't know its breed. Every twelfth year is the year of the dog. This means that people born in 1910, 1922, 1934, 1946, 1958, 1970, 1982, 1994, 2006, 2018 and 2030 are all born under the sign of the dog. According to Chinese astrologers, those born under the sign of the dog are said to be honest, loyal and champions of justice. They can also be stubborn, tend to worry too much, and are not fond of crowds or social gatherings. People born in the year of the dog tend to be successful as educators, writers, philosophers, doctors, scientists, judges, priests and of course, as critics.

Despite the dog's august astrological qualities, Mao Zedong banned them as pets in China during the Cultural Revolution of 1965. He stated that raising dogs was a "bourgeois pastime". This resulted in the extermination of millions of dogs. For many years the only way that a person living in China could get to see a Pekingese dog was to go to a zoo. In her book, *Beijing Confidential: A Tale of Comrades Lost and Found*, Jan Wong says, "After Mao's death, people began surreptitiously keeping dogs, although they remained illegal until the 1990s. The urban middle class had to content itself with renting them for ten-minute walks in special parks."

Fortunately times have changed and now there are huge pet stores in China and a Beijing kennel club. In fact, so many Chinese have decided to own pet dogs that in some regions a "one dog per family" law had to be passed. However, just as in the West, the Chinese dote over their dogs and treat them as cherished pets...completely ignoring their astrological potential to become writers, philosophers, doctors, scientists, judges and priests!

Dogs have played many roles during human warfare, some important and some minor. General George Washington, who became the first president of the United States, had a special fondness for dogs. Washington was avidly interested in fox hunting, so it is not surprising that his major interest was in hounds. With his usual painstaking care he began to build a pack of hunting hounds. They became his hobby, and his diaries are filled with his accounts of his dog breeding. Washington's feelings about these dogs can be detected in the names that he gave them. There was Sweetlips, Venus, and Truelove. These shared a kennel with dogs named Taster, Tippler and Drunkard, but we don't have time for a psychological analysis of other proclivities indicated by these names. After the American Revolutionary War, the French general, Marquis de Lafayette acknowledged Washington's passion by sending him a pack of five hounds as a gift.

Washington's affection for dogs is vividly illustrated in an incident that occurred during the war. It was when American forces were trying to contain British General William Howe's troops, who had occupied New York City. During the Battle of Long Island (which went badly for the Americans) General Howe's little terrier became lost between the lines. The dog was identified from its collar, and brought to Washington. He kept the dog in his tent while he fed him; afterwards he ordered a cease-fire. The shooting stopped and soldiers on both sides watched as one of Washington's aides formally returned a little dog to the British commander under a flag of truce.

During World War I, Colonel H.E. Richardson founded the first British dog school designed to train dogs for specialized military tasks. When the call for canine recruits went out the number of dogs "volunteered" by their owners was astounding. Nearly seven thousand dogs were offered to the army in the first two weeks following the announcement that dogs were needed for military service. This meant that Richardson needed some way to separate the dogs that would be best suited to be war-dogs from those less likely to be useful. Part of his selection criterion was based upon observation of the dog's tail. Colonel Richardson claimed that dogs that carry their tails curled jauntily over their backs rarely have any value for military purposes. "This method of carrying the tail seems to indicate a certain levity of character, quite a variance with the serious duties required."

In World War II the allies needed dogs for many purposes. In the United States alone, well over 50,000 dogs were enlisted and five War-Dog Reception and Training Centers were established by the U.S. Army Quartermaster Corps. The most common use for the dogs was in sentry work. However, dogs found themselves employed in many different jobs. Some were used to lay telephone wire, to carry packs, or to haul ammunition and guns. Some dogs served as scouts and even artillery or gun spotters. Some dogs continued their civilian chores, such as keeping the rat population down in army camps and in front line foxholes and trenches. Others were trained for delicate and dangerous tasks. This included mine detection. Dogs became especially important means of finding land mines after the Germans introduced non-metallic, plastic mines in North Africa, since these were completely invisible to traditional magnetic mine detectors.

Perhaps the most exotic occupation was held by the dogs that were trained as spies. They were taught to infiltrate enemy camps to steal documents. Despite advice like that from Colonel Richardson, the U.S. Army drafted all breeds of dogs. The only breed explicitly refused by war-dog recruiters was the basset hound.

Religious beliefs have also had their impact on the relationships between dogs and humans. Throughout Alaska and the Aleutian Island chain (which extends from Alaska out into the Bering Sea) there were a number of tribes that believed that their god, the creator of all living things, first came to earth in the form of a dog. It was believed that the first woman had ten children who were fathered by this dog. Five remained near where they were born and were the ancestors of all of the tribes of Indians, while the other five set to sea on a raft, and ultimately became all of the other people in the world.

Among almost all Indian tribes, prior to the arrival of the Europeans, dogs were the only draft animals. They were required to drag household items from place to place on a travois, a kind of primitive vehicle which consisted of two poles that were attached to a harness on the dog. The poles trailed on the ground behind the animals with a platform or basket strung between them. However, out of respect for the creator's dog form, at certain times in the year, the Chippewa Indians of Alaska would not use dogs for their usual transport and hauling functions. During those periods of time the dogs were allowed to run free while it was the women of the tribe who were required to pull the travois.

Women, dogs, and spiritual beliefs all mix in a strange custom found in Central India among certain of the Gond peoples. This leads to a ritual that actually accepts the marriage of a human being to a dog. The Gond are aboriginal tribes, that still speak a fairly obscure set of unwritten languages. Their lifestyle, while not truly nomadic, tends away from permanent settlements and villages are periodically moved to various sites on land communally owned by their clan. Their beliefs place them outside of the Hindu caste system. They do not acknowledge the superiority of Brahmans and don't feel bound by many Hindu rules. Especially in the highlands of Bastar, their style of agriculture is quite traditional, involving slash and burn operations. Because they are continually clearing wild land, the Gond often encounter wild animals, and these encounters can be fatal to humans armed only with digging sticks or hoes.

The Gond of Bastar believe that if a woman's husband has been killed by a wild animal, especially a tiger, it is necessary for her to marry a dog, before she can take another husband. The Gond believe that the dead husband's spirit now inhabits the tiger or other beast that killed him and this spirit will then cause that same beast to kill any new man that the woman marries. To solve this problem the widow first must ceremonially marry a dog. The dead husband's spirit can then satisfy his jealousy be killing the dog, and he will not threaten the life of the new human husband. While this seems like a good outcome for the woman, I think that dogs know that a simple divorce would be a better end of their marriage than the one the Gond envisions for them.

It is probably the case that few dogs know that there is a holiday set aside for them—the third of November, the feast day of Saint Hubert, the patron saint of dogs. Hubert was the son of the Belgian Duke of Guienne. As a young man, he was boisterous, self-indulgent and dearly loved to hunt. His redeeming grace was his love of dogs. The story is that he and some friends irreverently took their hounds out to hunt on Good Friday in 683 AD. During the hunt the dogs suddenly stopped their pursuit and reverently lay down in front a great white stage. When the stag turned Hubert saw the image of the cross between its antlers and heard the voice of God telling him that it was time to begin to hunt for virtue. Shortly thereafter Hubert took Holy Orders, established an abbey and eventually rose to be a bishop of the church. At the abbey he continued to breed dogs and created the Saint Hubert Hound, from which our modern Bloodhounds have descended.

One early November, some years ago, I was travelling through rural North Carolina. I stopped when I came upon a large crowd, standing in front of a church. The crowd consisted of all kinds of people and dogs: children with pets, shepherds with sheep dogs, and hunters with hounds. The priest mounted the church steps, dressed in white robes, and proceeded to give the "Mass of the Dogs" in honor or Saint Hubert. At the end the oldest dog was called up and blessed and then every dog in turn received a benedictory touch from the priest. I am certain that no dog present barked even once during the entire proceedings. Actually, according to my recollection, many dogs seemed to respectfully bow their heads during the prayer service.

For some reason there has always been a link between dogs and Christmas. Perhaps it's because the Christian account of the birth of Jesus has him surrounded by shepherds. Since shepherds require dogs it has become traditional to show dogs with the people gathered around the manger in nativity scenes. In Grenada, Spain, the tale is told about three dogs that followed the three shepherds into Bethlehem. When they found the infant Jesus the dogs were given the opportunity to gaze upon him and they were blessed by the holy infant's smile. The dog's names were "Cubilon", "Lubina" and "Melampo". It is for this reason that many people in Grenada still give their dogs these names in – sort of a good luck charm.

Lyndon Baines Johnson, former president of the United States, loved both dogs and Christmas. He even went so far as to have Christmas cards made up which featured a picture of him with two of his dogs, his white Collie, Blanco, and one of his Beagles, Him. The card was signed with Johnson's signature and the paw prints of the two dogs.

On his last Christmas in the White House, the presidential family gathered around the Christmas tree. The mood was light, despite the fact that the Democratic Party had been defeated in the last election and Richard Nixon, who Johnson despised, would soon be replacing him as president. Yuki, the president's well-loved white terrier, was decked out as Santa Claus, with a red coat and a proper hat. Yuki was sniffing around the tree and suddenly stopped and lifted his leg. Johnson laughed and removed a now wet box from the pile of gifts and announced, "I suppose that Santa has just told us which present he wants to give to President Nixon!"

Joan Dyck, of Chicago tells another holiday tale about her Shetland Sheepdog. "I suppose that she was meant to be a Christmas elf from the beginning. My husband gave her to me as a Christmas gift, so I named her 'Noel'. A year later, our daughter Rebecca was born. When Becky was around three and a half years old, we moved away from our center city apartment, to a real house. We could now have Christmas with a tree in front of a real fireplace. Becky was worried about whether Santa Claus would fit down the chimney, but we explained to her that Santa was magic, and could shrink himself down to elf size. We also warned her that she had to stay in her room, since Santa wouldn't give gifts to children if he saw them out of bed when he came. Christmas Eve came and when Becky was asleep we set up the tree. Around midnight Becky burst into our bedroom and woke us crying 'I saw Santa! Is he going to take away my presents now?' While her father comforted her I cautiously sneaked downstairs. There in the empty fireplace sat Noel, shaking a fancy red Christmas stocking in order to get some candies out of it. To sleepy little eyes here was Santa. That was 12 years ago and I have still found no need to tell Becky otherwise."

CHAPTER 7

What Do Dogs Do?

Dogs are not just kept as companions, but many dogs have jobs and specific functions. The dog's sense of loyalty and its natural instinct to defend its territory gives birth to term "watchdogs", and make the larger animals good guard dogs, able to intervene and protect property and people. Some—like the Doberman Pinscher, German Shepherd, or virtually any terrier—do not have to be trained to be watchdogs. These breeds will automatically sound the alarm at any disturbance near their home. Of course there will be false alarms as well, such as when the wind brushing against the house at 2 AM may trigger their guarding instincts and a burst of frantic warning noise. Experts say any list of the top dogs for watchdog barking should include: Rottweilers, German Shepherds, Doberman Pinschers, all terriers—from the large Airedale to the tiny Yorkshire Terrier, Schnauzers of all sizes, Poodles, Shih-Tzus and surprisingly the tiny Chihuahua who will loudly sound the alarm when any stranger approaches.

Other breeds take a more relaxed approach to watching or guarding. For instance, dogs like the Labrador Retriever know that the best watchdogs can guard the household simply by choosing some appropriate place to sleep. With the right choice, in the darkness, a burglar is bound to inadvertently trip over them with a loud clatter, thus alerting the family.

One day a man showed up at my university office with a video tape that he wanted me to see.

"I know that in one of your books you said that Chihuahuas were good watch dogs, and will bark to warn about anything unusual", he began. "On the other hand, you also said that they were no good as guard dogs since there was no way that such a little dog could actually physically protect you if someone was out to hurt you. Well the reason that I am here is that I want to show you that you were wrong.

"While I was in Mexico I visited a man who trains Chihuahuas as guard dogs." I watched with amazement as the video played. It showed a man wearing a padded suit, like that used to train attack dogs. He was acting the part of a thief and stealthily opening a garden gate. Suddenly a pack of about a dozen tiny dogs swarmed all over him, biting, slashing and barking."

"This is all very impressive, but wouldn't it be more efficient just to have one big Rottweiler or a Doberman Pinscher?" I asked.

"Not at all", was the reply. "It only takes one gunshot or a good hit with a club to disable a single big guard dog. With a pack of ten or more Chihuahuas the intruder can't stop them all. He wouldn't have enough bullets and they would incapacitate him before he could club every one of them. You see, they are trained to just keep biting and slashing, like a school of piranha fish."

I suppose that I had just learned a fact that dogs already know, namely that the important thing is not the size of the dog in a fight, but the size of the fight in the dog.

Dogs certainly know how to guard their masters, but sometimes they misinterpret threats. In 1530, King Henry VIII sent the Cardinal Thomas Wolsey to visit the Pope. The Cardinal had a petition requesting annulment of Henry's marriage to Catherine of Aragon. Henry wanted this annulment so that he could marry his newest heartthrob, Ann Boleyn. The Cardinal took his favorite Greyhound, named Urian, with him to the audience. When Wolsey knelt and the pontiff extended his foot so that he could kiss his toe, as was the custom at the time, the Urian interpreted this as an attempt to kick his master's face. The dog immediately leapt forward and protectively bit the holy digits.

Given the havoc that ensued it is not surprising that the divorce was not granted. As a result, Henry VIII broke away from the Catholic Church and formed the Church of England. He then appointed Thomas Cranmer as the Archbishop of Canterbury, and, perhaps unsurprisingly, this eminent cleric had a much more liberal attitude toward granting him freedom from his wife.

Dogs do many things to help people. One of their most unusual functions involves assisting in psychotherapy. This all started with Sigmund Freud, who had a series of dogs, most of them Chow Chows. Freud felt that dogs had a special sense that allows them to accurately judge a person's character. For this reason his favorite Chow Chow, Jo-Fi, attended many of his therapy sessions. Freud felt that with the dog in the room his patients, especially the children, felt more relaxed and more freely communicated with him. Freud also admitted that he often depended upon Jo-Fi for an assessment the patient's mental state.

More recent studies have shown that Freud was correct. Physiological measures show that petting a calm and friendly dog does actually reduce stress. This shows up as reduced muscle tension, more regular breathing and a slower heart rate. There is even some evidence that people who own dogs are likely to live longer and require less medical attention. Freud's dog Jo-Fi would alert him to any stress or tension in a patient by where he laid down during the session. He would lie relatively near to calm patients, but would stay across the room if the patient was tense.

Jo-Fi also helped the great psychoanalyst determine when a therapy session was finished. Without fail, he would get up and move towards the office door when the hour was ended. Freud, however, insisted that the rumor that Jo-Fi actually did the therapeutic psychoanalysis and wrote up the case reports is false.

In most places in the Western World, laws only acknowledge the value of dogs as mere property. One newspaper article, for example, reported the case of one Else Brown, a widow aged 67 years. Her dog, Tilley, was her only life companion. Tragically, a neighbor killed Tilley in a drunken act of aggression. The court ruled that this was not an assault, but just a crime against property, which would be treated like simple vandalism—the equivalent of breaking a window. Thus Tilley's murderer was simply given a fine equal to the cost of the dog. The total was just a pitiful few dollars since she had been adopted from an animal shelter.

The years of love and caring, the loss of companionship had no dollar value in the eyes of the law. Dogs know that you can buy them if you have enough money. However it will take more than money to compensate for their companionship and the wag of their tails.

Even as property, though, dogs have influenced many aspects of history. Just about everyone knows the story of Jamestown, the first permanent British settlement in Virginia. We tend to think of it as the story of the Indian maiden Pocahontas. The fact that the settlement survived is really also is a story about dogs, not as companions, but as trade goods.

Jamestown was founded in 1607 but was viciously attacked by the Algonquin Indians and nearly half the colonists were dead in the first six months. The colony was saved by several events. The first was the well-known event where Pocahontas intervened to save Captain John Smith from execution by her father, Chief Powhatan. The second was the arrival of supply ship containing 100 fresh settlers, much needed food, tools and of equal importance dogs. The British wanted gold, which had been discovered in the nearby Carolinas and Georgia. They also wanted fur, tobacco and Indian corn. The colonists found that they had an item that the Indians would gladly trade for, namely British hunting dogs. Good hunting dogs were considered much more precious than gold by the Indians since they had not yet mastered the technique of specialized dog breeding for hunting skills. The dogs became such a major consideration that they were specifically mentioned in the 1657 treaty that ended the conflict between Powhatan's Algonquins and the colonists. The central role of dogs in forging the peace is still celebrated by a dog parade, and canine sports events at the annual October Dog Mart Day in Fredericksburg Virginia, although it seems to have been overlooked in the recent Hollywood films about Pocahontas.

Dogs know that they are often prized for some completely utilitarian reasons. For example, in North America, prior to the arrival of the Europeans, there were no domestic sheep. The northwestern coastal Indians, therefore, developed a remarkably shaggy breed of dog, simply for its fur. This fur was very soft and warm and was mixed with fur shed by wild goats or with eiderdown or pounded cedar bark. When this mixture was spun, it could be used to make soft, warm, blankets and clothing. The British explorer, Captain George Vancouver, reported that in 1798, when he entered Puget Sound in what is now the state of Washington, he was greeted by a pack of these dogs "all shorn as close to the skin as sheep are in England. So compact were their fleeces that large portions could be lifted up by a corner without causing any separation." Such dogs were often kept on small islands or penned in some way, in order to prevent them from breeding with other dogs, whose fur was of lesser quality. Unfortunately, these "wool dogs" were put out of business by the Hudson's Bay Company, when they introduced the Indians to mass-produced woolen trade blankets.

Edith Wharton, the Pulitzer Prize winning novelist who created classics like *Ethan Frome*, was once asked to make a list of the passions that ruled her life. First on this list was "Justice and Order" and second was "Dogs". Dogs, of course, are sometimes a great aid in maintaining justice and order, working as patrol dogs and drug detecting dogs. Sometimes, however, they end up on the wrong side of the law.

A visiting scholar told me a story about his father. He lived in Hamburg, Germany, where well-trained guard and companion dogs are sought after and can sell for very high prices. "My father was fond of German Shepherds and had heard that there was a dog trainer and breeder named Hans Roehm who had splendid dogs. When he went to see Roehm, he was quite impressed, and bought a dog named Max from him. Max was very expensive, but he was very handsome and completely trained. Max had been with Father for only a week when he disappeared. Apparently he had run away. Advertisements in the paper had no success in finding the dog. Then, about a month later, my father saw a dog that looked exactly like Max. He stopped the owner and found out that this dog had also been purchased from Hans Roehm. When Father called Roehm he was told that that dog was a litter mate of Max's, which was why his markings were so similar. Another month passed and Father again met the man who owned Max's brother. He did not have the dog with him since it turns out that the dog had run away! Father was suspicious and contacted the police. An investigation found that Roehm was a very fine trainer indeed. He had trained his dogs to escape back to him as soon as they had a chance. Max had actually been sold nine times to nine different people!"

Sometimes it the dog, himself, that ends up in court. In 1976, in Grand Prairie, Texas, a six-year-old Schnauzer, also named Max, was put on trial. He was charged with breaking and entering and he was also charged with the rape of two pedigreed Pekingese females, named Dollie and Sen-Lee. Charges were brought by Dollie and Sen-Lee's owner, George Milton. He was suing for damage to his house and for veterinarian fees, to cover the abortions that were required after the assault. The judge, Cameron Grey, decided that Max was not guilty. He cited, as the basis of this ruling, the fact that the police had held a line up to identify the molester. At that time, Mr. Milton had confidently singled out a Poodle as the assailant of his tiny dogs.

Sometimes both dog and owner end up in court. In 1996, in Waterbury, Connecticut, a local political activist named Barbary Monsky sued Judge Howard Moraghan and his Golden Retriever Kodak, for sexual harassment. Moraghan often brought his dog to Dansbury Superior Court. According to Monsky the dog had "nuzzled, snooped or sniffed" beneath her skirt at least three times, while the judge had done nothing about it. U.S. District Judge Gerard Goettel dismissed the case, and in a later interview explained that, "Impoliteness on the part of a dog does not constitute sexual harassment on the part of the owner." The aggrieved woman responded by calling that decision "as insulting as having a dog sniff under a skirt."

24 percent of dogs received formal obedience training and about two out of three successfully completed the course.

CHAPTER 8

How Do Dogs Learn?

Dogs do learn. There is an old folk proverb that goes "Experience is the best teacher, and fools will have no other". Perhaps this is why some people think that dogs are lamentably crude or ignorant, simply because their total experience with life has been drawn from life itself. As dogs grow older their behavior does show that they have learned from their experiences. They become shrewder, more perceptive and perhaps a bit cunning. They develop the capacity to judge and evaluate certain situations much more accurately. Thus for dogs, it is clear that judgment comes from experience, however experience comes mostly from bad judgments. Dogs know that a life spent making mistakes is a lot more honorable than a life spent doing nothing at all.

I recently received a card in which informed me "We certainly live a strange world, where kids run wild in the streets and dogs go to obedience classes." Dog obedience classes are quite common, and they are probably the closest thing to formal education that most dogs will ever encounter. While it may be hard to tell how intelligent dogs are, a recent survey looked at how many dogs have gone to "school". Only 24 percent of all dogs were ever given any formal obedience training. How well did this schooling work? Well, one out of every three dog owners say that their

pet either flunked out of the class, or that they gave up before the class was over.

For dogs that do well in obedience training there are many opportunities to display their education. Most major kennel clubs have dog obedience competitions where the dog can display its proficiency and knowledge. In North America dogs can earn three different obedience degrees. The CD stands for Companion Dog, and this degree requires the dog to perform basic exercises that all civilized dogs should be capable of, such as responding to "sit", "down" and "stay" commands, coming when called, and walking beside their master in a controlled manner. The CDX or Companion Dog Excellent degree, requires the dog to obey off leash, and adds tasks like jumping and retrieving on command. The highest degree is the UD or Utility Dog, requires sophisticated behaviors, like responding to hand signals instead of spoken commands, and finding and retrieving items by scent alone. One dog obedience judge admitted to me that sometimes, at a practical level, it is difficult to know whether a dog that won't sit, come, or fetch on command, is too stupid to learn or too smart to bother.

It is difficult to know the overall goals or plans that guide any particular dog's behavior. One woman told me that her dog Bullet, a retriever of sorts, engaged in very systematic behaviors that seemed to make no sense to her as a human being. Because she was tired of tripping over Bullet's toys, she had gathered together all of his dog toys and put them in a box in one corner of her kitchen. As she expected, during the afternoon Bullet took out various toys to play with. At the end of the day, however, she found all of the toys neatly piled in a corner of the living room. Feeling that this was Bullet's way of suggesting where he wanted his toy box to be located, she moved the container to that corner. The next evening she found the toys stacked in yet a different corner. Thinking that the problem might be the box itself, she left the pile of toys where the dog had put them. The next night the toys had been moved to yet another corner. "I stopped worrying about the whereabouts of his toys. Each night he moves them somewhere else, but at least, now, they are always neatly stacked." What she had missed was the fact that dogs believe that activity and movement is more important than plans or goals. Action is always preferable to inaction even if the acts are without a specific guiding principal. In other words, dogs don't quite know where they are going, but they do know that they are on their way.

When dogs know something, they usually do not consider alternative interpretations. For example, during World War II, the Germans trained their military dogs to respond to certain hand signals. One of these was the traditional command for "halt", involving an extended arm with the palm outward. There is a report that after Hitler assumed power, trained army dogs were part of a military parade that passed him in review. As the dog handlers approached, the Fuhrer gave the Nazi salute. The obedient dogs saw what they believed to be a familiar signal and immediately responded according to their training by sitting down. Of course, the troops immediately behind, who were moving with their eyes rigidly facing forward in the German marching style, promptly stumbled over them, resulting in a chaotic pile of dogs and people. The dog handlers were so embarrassed that they were forced to retrain the dogs to a new signal.

Whether dogs know it or not, they often rely more upon instinct than upon knowledge or education. The Nazis stationed along the Maginot Line used dogs as messengers. The French soldiers tried to shoot these dogs, but they moved very quickly and silently and were difficult to hit. One French dog handler then tried an experiment; he released a small female French messenger dog, which had just gone into heat. As she had been taught, later that evening the French dog returned to her post. Trailing behind her were nearly a dozen normally obedient German military dogs that had discovered an instinct which was much more powerful than their military training.

Dogs also know how to adapt to their environment. For example, dogs are smart enough to learn how to change their behavior to allow them to fit into a multicultural world. They are quite accepting of many points of view, and are neither racist, sexist nor even speciesist. This was proven by Marvin Goldman, of Brooklyn, New York, who brought home a young puppy, named Willy. In his home he also had a female cat that had just had a litter of kittens. His cat "adopted" Willy, treating him like one of her kittens, even to the point of washing him with her tongue. Willy responded by quickly learning cat culture, including the familiar cat habit of washing his paws with his tongue and then using them to clean his face and ears.

I am often bothered by my own limited knowledge. I don't speak French, Russian, or Italian even well enough to be able to adequately pronounce common words drawn from those languages or names people from places where these are spoken. This linguistic ignorance makes me feel uncomfortable around well-travelled people who know other tongues. There are whole areas in which any knowledge I may have ever acquired has long fled. I do not remember much physics, chemistry or astronomy. I can't tell the difference between a quark and a quirk, and all that I know about black holes is that things disappear inside of them, something like the way single socks disappear in the laundry. This lack of information makes me ill at ease around more technologically oriented scientists. My knowledge in the humanities and arts is also limited. I know little of the history of the British novel, I have memorized no Shakespearean sonnets, I cannot name any Flemish Renaissance portrait artists, nor do I remember who came first, Leonardo Da Vinci or Michelangelo. This makes me self-conscious around my more artistic acquaintances. My dogs, however, are quite comfortable around everybody. It may well be the case that the saving grace of dogs is that they don't know how much they don't know.

CHAPTER 9

Where Do Dogs Go?

Eventually all dogs, like all humans, do reach the end of their journey. A letter from a friend read "You know that she was just a four-footed ball of fluff with a high pitched bark at one end and bad manners at the other. I suppose that it is best that she didn't know how hard it would be on me when she went away since she used to get very upset when I was unhappy. She was, after all, only an animal, so the depth of my own feelings surprised me. It was as if, with her going, she was carrying away with her so many years of my life. I suppose that what finally pulled me out of my depression was religion. I spoke to a priest about what I was feeling and he said to me, 'Don't grieve so. You must always remember that as far as the Bible is concerned, God only threw the humans out of Paradise.'"

Are there dogs in Heaven? For those who love dogs it would be the worst form of a lie to call any place where dogs were banned "Paradise." Certainly no loving God separates people from their canine friends for eternity.

Robert Louis Stevenson, author of novels such as *Treasure Island*, declared, "You think dogs will not be in heaven? I tell you, they will be there before any of us."

The English writer of *Middlemarch* and *Adam Bebe*, George Eliot asked, "Shall we, because we walk on our hind feet, assume to ourselves only the privilege of

imperishability? Shall we, who are even as they, though
we wag our tongues and not our tails, demand a special
Providence and a selfish salvation?"

Then there was Saint Patrick, the patron saint of Ireland.
Tradition says that he promised Oissain, the son of the great
hero Finn Mac Cumhail, that for helping him Christianize
the land he could have his hounds in heaven.

Martin Luther, founder of the Protestant church was
once asked by his daughter Mary whether her dog, Topol,
would be allowed in heaven. He gently patted the dog's head
and said, "Be comforted, little dog. Come the resurrection
even thee shall wear a golden tail."

Entrance to heaven is likely not breed-specific, although
some dogs may likely have a bit more baggage on their
journey there. In his book *Three Men in a Boat (To Say
Nothing of the Dog)*, English author Jerome K. Jerome muses
that "fox-terriers are born with about four times as much
original sin in them as other dogs are". That said, we can
take comfort from the title of the popular movie franchise
"All Dogs Go To Heaven".

Shortly after my old Cairn Terrier, Flint, died I had
a dream. In it Flint was lying beside the gates of Heaven
and an angel came out to ask him why he didn't come in.
In the thought talk, given only to celestial beings, my dog
answered, "Can't I just stay out here awhile? I'll be good and
I won't even bark. You see I'm waiting for someone that I
miss very much. If I went in alone it wouldn't be heaven for
me." I woke from that dream to find tears on my face.

In many places around the world, there is a belief that
a dog's howl is a warning of a coming death. Some say that
this dire signal only occurs at midnight. Others say that
this death howl is quite unique, with the dog holding his
head down instead of pointed toward the sky as in the usual

howl. There are many who believe that a howling dog can actually drive the angel of death away. That would mean that the howling dog is trying to prevent the death that it sees coming.

In many religions dogs are psychopomps. That means that when you die it is a dog's job to escort you to the next world, and to protect you and show the way. Yima, the Zoroastrian god, has set two four-eyed dogs to guard Chinvat Bridge, which is known as the "Bridge of Decision" between this world and heaven. These dogs are placed there because they, like all dogs, are good judges of character. It is said that they will not let anyone pass on to Paradise if they have deliberately harmed a dog in this world.

Dogs don't know about beginnings and never speculate on matters that occurred before their time. Dogs also don't know, or at least don't accept, the concept of death. Everyone probably knows the story of Greyfriar's Bobby, the little Skye Terrier in Edinburgh, Scotland, who would not admit the death of his master. After the funeral he would not leave the gravesite, and for the next 9 years, he faithfully returned everyday to lie by his master's resting place.

Greyfriar's Bobby is not alone. Hachiko was an Akita owned by Dr. Eisaburo Ueno, a professor at Tokyo University. Hachiko accompanied his master to the train station each day to see him off. He would return to the station each afternoon to greet his master. One afternoon Professor Ueno did not return—he had died in Tokyo. Hachiko waited at the station until midnight. The next day, and every day for nearly 10 years thereafter, Hachiko came to the station and waited for his master. After the train came, and the passengers dispersed Hachiko would search the station carefully, before walking, slowly, home alone. With no concept of beginnings or endings, dogs probably don't know that for people, having a dog as a life companion provides a brief streak of light between two eternities of darkness.

Dogs seem to be tuned to sense the elusive essence of what we call life. Take the case of Mickey and Percy. Mickey was a Labrador retriever owned by William Harrison and Percy was a Chihuahua that had been given to his daughter Christine. Despite their size difference, the two dogs were good friends and playmates until one evening in 1983 when Percy ran out into the street and was hit by a car. While Christine stood by weeping, her father placed the dead dog in a crumpled sack and buried him in a shallow grave in the garden. The depression that had fallen on the family seemed to affect, not only the humans, but also Mickey, who sat despondently staring at the grave while everyone else went to bed.

A couple of hours later William was awakened by frantic whining and scuffling outside the house. When he investigated the noise he saw, to his horror, that the sack that he had buried Percy was now laying empty beside the opened grave. Next to it he saw Mickey, who was in a state of great agitation, standing over Percy's body frantically licking his face, nuzzling and poking at the limp form in what looked like a canine attempt to give the dead dog the kiss of life. Tears filled the man's eyes as he watched this futile expression of hope and love.

He sadly walked over to move Mickey away when he saw, what looked like a spasm or twitch. Then Percy weakly lifted his head and whimpered. Some deep sense in Mickey had sensed that there was a faint spark of life in the little dog, and his instinct to oppose death had told him what to do. For this act the animal charity Pro-dog named Mickey its Pet of the Year.

Marsha Hamilton's Golden Retriever, Buzzby, had been a vital part of her life for eleven years. Marsha often said that she couldn't have made it without Buzzby. When she had the miscarriage that had ended her dreams of being a mother, Buzzby had stayed at home and comforted her. When her marriage broke up Buzzby had been her "therapist" and confidant. Buzzby's emotional support got her through the hard times when she went back to university to study commercial art, and later during the depressing search for permanent employment. Then, just a few months after she finally got the job that she had dreamed about, Buzzby had died.

Marsha had barely begun to cope with this loss when a freak accident put her in the hospital. She had been involved in a multi-vehicle highway accident that had caused a truck carrying caustic chemicals to spill over her. She lay in the hospital, her face completely bandaged, an air vent down her mouth. No one could tell her whether her eyes were permanently damaged, or whether she would be able to talk normally again. Marsha was afraid. She really needed Buzzby's help now.

On the second night she felt a great weight settle beside her in bed. Her unbandaged left-hand reached out and felt familiar long fur. It was a Golden Retriever, so much like Buzzby that she almost cried. He came for three nights and she felt comforted and secure. On the next day doctors removed the bandages and Marsha found that she could see. As soon as she could speak again she asked whether she could see the dog that they had brought to her for visits. When she was told that there had been no dog, Marsha began to cry. She knew in her heart that Buzzby had come back to help her one last time, when she needed him most.

CHAPTER 10

Do Dogs Know People?

Dogs do understand people. In many respects they know humans better than other humans do. For example, dogs know that if they forgive a person enough they belong to that person and that person belongs to them. This happens without any thought and whether either party likes it or not. It is a cosmic law called "Squatters rights of the heart".

Dogs must be forgiving to live with such a fickle species as we are. Take the case of the Pit Bull Terrier. Before World War I, the Pit Bull Terrier was America's symbol of independent strength and security, and his picture appeared on posters declaring "Neutrality Without Fear". Pit Bulls were funny dogs, and were supposed to have a sense of humor. Everybody laughed at Petey, the Pit Bull that was one of the stars of the "Lil' Rascals" movies. Nice people owned Pit Bulls, including: Fred Astaire, Helen Keller, John Steinbeck and James Thurber. Of course there were occasional incidents, such as once, before the Ivy League was formed, when Princeton was playing football against Navy. During the halftime a person dressed as a Tiger (Princeton's mascot) was dancing around the field when Navy's mascot—a Pit Bull—was released and immediately dashed over to the prancing Tiger and tore off his tail. However, everybody knew that that was all in fun and did no permanent damage.

All of that has now changed. Today, fuelled by lurid press accounts of dog attacks, this type of dog is in danger of being legislated out of existence. Laws against these dogs often specify "Pit Bull or Pit Bull-like dogs," and this is interpreted to mean any dog with a large square head. One man told me that Animal Control Officers came to his home citing reports that he walked his Pit Bulls around his neighborhood without the muzzle required by municipal legislation. He protested, showing them his two dogs: a Boxer and a wrinkly Chinese Shar-Pei. These officials could not be convinced that these dogs did not fit into the Pit Bull category until they received a letter from his veterinarian.

A more egregious case of misidentification comes from Irvine, California, where three men stole two "Pit Bulls" from an animal shelter. Their idea was to sell these tough dogs to some criminals who ran an illegal dog-fighting operation. When they brought the dogs into a veterinarian for their vaccination shots, much to their surprise the dogs were identified as Chihuahuas! Microchips in the dog's ears also proved that these were stolen dogs. The thieves now have plenty of free time—in their jail cells—to learn how to identify different dog breeds!

Dogs forgive the fact that human love is fleeting. Back in 1931, in Newport Beach, California, there was a 150-pound Saint Bernard named Prince Pluto. Pluto would often go to the pier with his master, Richard Gunther, and then wander along the beach and socialize with the bathers who were there to enjoy the sun and waves. On that particular day, six-year-old George Mades was playing at ocean's edge. He had strayed from his parent's sight, and suddenly was caught by a series of large waves and dragged out into the deep water. The floundering child caught Pluto's eye, and in a moment the big, strong-swimming dog dashed into the water. Young George, despite his frantic flailing, was being drawn further from shore. When Pluto reached him, the child desperately grabbed at the dog, but missed. Pluto in turn, latched on to the boy's swimming trunks and started dragging him to shore. A few moments later the child managed to climb onto the dog's back. Struggling, the great dog worked his way back to shore. When George's parents reached the scene, the terrified little boy's fingers had to be forcefully peeled from the dog's fur.

This, however, was not the first time that Pluto had saved a child from drowning—it was the fifth time! For his heroism in the saving of five lives, Prince Pluto was named "Official Lifeguard of Newport Beach" by the city council. He was given a department badge and a safety light attached to a harness for protection from traffic, should he choose to make his rounds at night. He was also given the Latham Foundation's Gold Medal Award for animal heroism. Today, however, should you visit the site of Pluto's heroic activities, you will be greeted by a large sign reading "No Dogs Permitted On This Beach". Times change...

Still, of all of the animals, dogs are very special to us. One proof of this is that we only name special animals. Few farmers will name their beef cows, chickens or sheep. To name an animal is to grant it an identity and a uniqueness, and to accept it as a friend or companion. According to a recent survey the top 10 dog names in the English-speaking world are:

	Males	**Females**
1	Max	Molly
2	Jake	Bella
3	Buddy	Daisy
4	Jack	Maggie
5	Cody	Lucy
6	Charlie	Ginger
7	Bailey	Bonnie
8	Rocky	Sadie
9	Sam	Sophie
10	Buster	Lady

One surprise was that the name Snoopy—the dog made famous by Charles Schultz's comic strip *Peanuts*—was not in the top of the dog list; however it was found in the top 10 names for cats!

Some people name dogs for unique reasons. I was told of one woman who named her dog Banjo. It seems that her husband wanted a banjo to play folk music and had been hinting that it would make a great birthday present. She was worried because she knew that he had absolutely no musical talent. So she hit upon the plan to buy him the dog and gave it to him saying, "Now you have your own Banjo!"

A dog's name becomes a signal that tells it that the next sounds that come out of its master's mouth are supposed to have some impact on the dog's life. For instance, all of my dogs have two names. The first is their unique and solely owned name, like Wiz, Dancer or Odin, and the second is "Puppy". Thus when I yell "Puppies come" I expect all of my dogs within earshot to appear at a run.

Some other people's dogs have a more difficult time with their names. Consider the case of the Skye Terrier owned by Robert Louis Stevenson. Stevenson is best known for writing such classics as Treasure Island and The Strange Case of Dr. Jekyll and Mr. Hyde. His poor little dog was initially named "Woggs", which was then changed to "Walter", and then changed again to "Watty", then changed once more to "Woggy" and finally changed to "Bogue".

Most dogs do not have such problems in identifying themselves. The vast majority of dogs in the world know their names quite well based on its frequency of use and the variety of situations in which it occurs. If you asked most dogs what their name is they would tell you that it is "No!"

Dogs know that they eventually become a true member of their human family. They don't require any evidence for this, however, researchers like to explore just how much of a family member dogs become. One bit of proof comes from the fact that 38 percent of all dog owners admit that they have occasionally slipped and called their spouse by their dog's name. It is interesting to note that 25 percent of this same group has made a mistake in the opposite direction, calling their dog by their spouse's name. Women are most likely to make these particular errors, which may indicate that women see less of difference between their dog and their spouse than do men. It is interesting to note that children seem to be much more distinguishable than their parents. Only 11 percent of pet owners admitted to ever having called their children by their dog's name.

Dogs know that their owners often view them as if they were children. Great care is taken with their upkeep and grooming, including (as with kids) making sure that they are dressed appropriately for the weather and for social events. Surveys show that 86 percent of dog owners admit that they sometimes adorn their dogs with scarves or ribbons. Sixty-two percent of dog owners admit that their dog owns a sweater, winter coat, or raincoat...some own all three!

As for dress-up times, 23 percent of owners say that they own a fancy leash or collar, with jewels, sparkles or fancy embroidery, while 6 percent of dog owners say that they have occasionally put jewelry of other sorts on their dogs. I have difficulty conceptualizing what this "other jewelry" might be. I certainly refuse to put a gold earring on my spaniel, regardless of the fashion statement that it might make.

Another way that dogs are treated as children is seen when marriages break up. In 38 percent of divorce proceedings involving dog owners, neither party wanted to give up their four-legged "child". Sometimes the dispute over the dog turns into an extended and costly court battle. When the final decision is announced, just as in cases involving human children, judges seem predisposed to grant custody to the woman, with 81 percent of the rulings going in favor of the former wife. Furthermore, when women won custody of the dog, their former spouses were granted visiting rights in a meager 11 percent of the cases.

In those rare cases where the former husband was granted custody of the dog, however, their ex-wife was granted visitation rights in 83 percent of the proceedings.

While on the subject of being separated from one's dog, according to Harper's Index, it is estimated that more than one million Americans have named their dogs as beneficiaries in their wills.

People know the depth of the bond between dogs and humans. It is felt in the heart each time our dog comes to us when we call it, or lies next to us simply because it wants to share our company. Many cultures have stories of how humans and dogs came to be together. My favorite is found in the tales of several tribes of American Plains Indians. It tells of a time long ago, when God, the Great Spirit, had just finished creating the world and all of its inhabitants. Then the Great Spirit decided that it was time to separate the world of humans from the world of animals. He sent out a call to gather all of the living creatures on a wide plain. When they had assembled he drew a line in the ground. On one side of this line were humans, on the other were all of the other animals. Now, while everyone watched, the line began to deepen and widen. It became a great crack in the earth. Then this crack began to open and a bottomless chasm began to form. The abyss continued to widen, and then, at the last moment, just before the gap became unbreachable—dog leapt over to stand by man.

The Nobel Prize winning author Maurice Maeterlinck expressed these same feelings when he said, "We are alone, absolutely alone on this chance planet; and amid all the forms of life that surround us, not one, excepting the dog, has made an alliance with us."

Dogs can only know what they can sense and this is ultimately their saving grace. Some psychologists say that it may well be that the origin of modern neurosis in people began with the discoveries of Copernicus. They say that this neurosis came about because Science made humans feel small. It did this by showing people that the Earth is not the center of the universe and it is only a tiny speck floating in an immense void. Science further attacked people's self-image by proposing the Theory of Evolution, which suggests that humans not only are somehow related to apes, but also in the more distant past we have relatives who were insects and even sea slime. Dogs are unaffected by these revelations simply because they don't care. Dogs have opted never to inquire "Why?", "How?" or to ask whether. A dog's philosophy is simply to enjoy his food while it is on his plate.

Dogs may not know, or care, about the full extent of their own limitations; however, after years of carefully observing human beings, they certainly seem to know ours.

One day my dog came over to me while I was working. He looked at me and seemed to say, "It is all very well to be able to write books, but can you waggle your ears?"

So can we total things up and determine and assess the wisdom of dogs in order to reveal what dogs really know? Probably not in a manner that a scientist or even a philosopher would accept. We may never be able to fully understand how dogs see the world. We may never determine what dogs know about humans or why dogs find our species to be so special. We may never understand what drives dogs to spend much of their lives doing things that they put humans in asylums for. We may also live our lives never comprehending why, impelled by a state of mind that is not to last, dogs often make irrevocable decisions. Science may never fully comprehend the full extent of what dogs know about language, problem solving, the past, the future, God, time or philosophy.

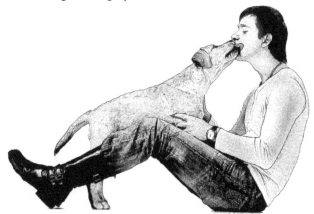

In the end we must content ourselves with the fact that dogs are wise enough to know how to be dogs—which is all that is really required of them.

🐾🐾

Lightning Source UK Ltd.
Milton Keynes UK
UKHW040603231219
355886UK00001B/54/P

9 780973 105292